LET'S PATTERN BLOCK IT

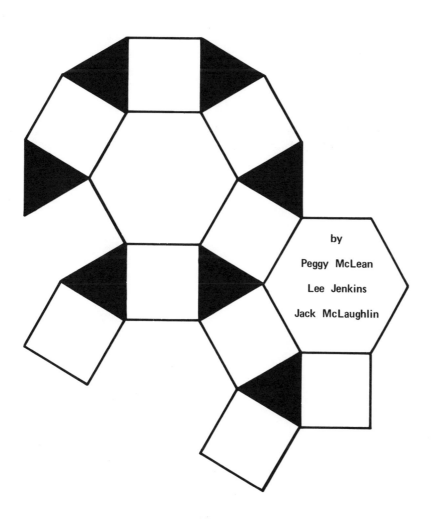

by

Peggy McLean

Lee Jenkins

Jack McLaughlin

Published by

ACTIVITY RESOURCES COMPANY, INC.

P.O. Box 4875

Hayward, California 94540

Copyright ©1973
Activity Resources Company, Inc.
P.O. Box 4875
Hayward, California 94540

Typeset by Vera Allen Composition Service, Hayward, California.

TABLE OF CONTENTS

PUBLICATIONS BY ACTIVITY RESOURCES COMPANY, INC.

RESOURCE BOOKS

The Fabric of Mathematics (K-8)
The Tapestry of Mathematics (7-12)
The Correlations of Activity
   Centered Science and Mathematics (K-8)

MATH IS EVERYWHERE SERIES (K-8)

Laboratory Laughter (Science)
Mathematical Manka (Literature)
Math and Art (Art)
Sports (Physical Education)
Word Ways (Language Arts)

MANIPULATIVES AND HOW TO USE THEM

Algebra in Concrete (5-9)
Attribute Acrobatics (1-6)
Base Ten Mathematics (1-8)
Coin Stamp Mathematics (1-4)
Colored Cube Activity Cards (K-3)
Fraction Tile Program (1-9)
Geoblocks and Geojackets (3-10)
Let's Pattern Block It (K-8)
Math Balance Book (1-4)
Metric Multibase Mathematics (1-10)
Number Triangles (5-11)

METRIC BOOKS

Do Decimals First (3-9)
Making Metric Maneuvers (2-6)
The Merry Metric Cookbook (K-3)
The Metric System of Measurement (5-9)
Metrics All Around (2-6)

MATH ART

Mathmagic with Flexagons (3 up)
The Maze Book (1-6)
Pholdit (1 up)

TASK CARDS

Climate in 3-D (4-9)
Environmental Geometry (K-8)
Zoom (K-3)

GAMES (K-8)

Enhance Chance
Friendly Games to Make and Learn
Games and Aids for Teaching Math
Math Fold A Game
Place Value and Regrouping Games
Tripletts
Ready-to-Play Multiplication and Division Games

SOCIAL STUDIES AND READING

Springboard (1-6)
Shape Book (K-4)

ACTIVITY BOOKS

Calculators, Number Patterns, and Magic (3-12)
Focus on Decimals 1, 2 (4-9)
Focus on Fractions 1, 2, 3 (3-8)
Graphiti (3-12)
Holiday Mathemagic (4-10)
Puzzling Your Way Into Geometry (6-10)
Skeletons, Word Problems, and Dinosaurs
   (8-11)

DIRECTIONS

These pages were designed to be used by the child with pattern blocks available to him.

The pages can be used as a task card or ditto master. Using the page as a ditto master provides each child with his own page on which to record.

Pattern block stickers are available to add color to the task card approach.

GEOMETRY (Pages 1 — 9)

The purpose of these pages is to introduce the pattern blocks to the students.

MATRICES (Pages 10 — 13)

The purpose of these pages is to teach a child how to read a matrix. Most children need assistance on pages 10 and 11. Pictured below are acceptable answers.

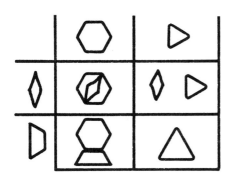

COUNTING (Pages 14 — 16)

These pages are necessary for learning the area values of the blocks when the green triangle equals 1. A strategy for children would be to see how many green triangles each shape holds.

EQUIVALENCE (Page 17)

This is the first in a series of equivalence puzzles presented throughout the book. Have the child cover the shape with his own selection of blocks. He counts and records the number of blocks used on the page by circling the numeral. The strategy of these pages is to find the maximum and minimum number of blocks possible and to realize that all numbers in between are possible.

GEOMETRIC COVER TASKS (Pages 18 — 27)

These pages are designed to develop in children the necessary strategies for the more difficult tasks to follow (like area, perimeter, fractions, place value and symmetry).

ADDITION (Pages 29 — 31)

Give the child 10 orange squares. Have him put them on the X's on pages 29 and 30. The child should write the number sentence for the horizontal and vertical problems he sees.

Page 31 requires the child to place the 10 blocks anywhere he chooses and write the two number sentences. Provide several copies of page 31 for each child.

INEQUALITIES (Pages 34 — 38)

The child selects the letter of the smallest shape and then ranks the remaining shapes. If he is correct he spells one of the pattern block colors.

PATTERN DEVELOPMENT (Pages 39 — 42)

These pages on tesselations ask children to continue a pattern that is started. Children will appreciate the beauty of these repeating patterns.

SEQUENCES (Pages 44 — 56)

The child is asked to discover the pattern and complete it.

ADDITION (pages 57 — 59)

The child should circle the numbers he can make using any combination of the pieces allowed for each problem.

TIME (Pages 60 — 62)

These pages are enrichment for children who can accurately tell time.

PATTERN NUMERALS (Pages 63 — 66)

All of these numerals can be made with the pattern blocks.

CLASSIFICATION (Pages 67 — 76)

Pages 67 — 71 require children to determine which attribute describes the set. For example on page 67 "eggys" have hexagons. On page 72 the title of each set is given. On pages 73 — 76 the child must write his own title and classify the objects under his own titles.

SYMMETRY (Pages 77 — 97)

For pages 77 and 78, have the child place the blocks on the shapes and the mirror on the line facing the blocks. The task is to build with blocks the image that he sees in the mirror.

For pages 79–81, have the child place the blocks on the drawn shape and the mirror on the line facing the blocks. The task is to build with the blocks the image that he sees in the mirror.

For pages 82–88, 90 have the child place the blocks on the drawn shape and the mirror on both arrows. The task is to determine if the mirror image is the same as the other half of the figure. On page 82 the first two figures have mirror symmetry and the third figure does not.

For pages 89 and 91 the child must place the mirror on each of the sets of arrows in sequence. The task is to circle the number of lines of symmetry.

Page 92 introduces rotational symmetry. Have the child place the blocks on the drawn figure. He must rotate all the blocks together so that the blocks formerly at the top of the figure are now at the bottom. If after rotating the blocks the pattern is still the same the shape has rotational symmetry.

Page 93 requires the child to rotate the blocks twice. After the first rotation the block originally touching point A is at point B. After the second rotation the block originally at point A is at point C.

Pages 94 and 95 require the child to rotate the blocks 5 times.

For pages 96 and 97 the child must meet the three requirements listed below for each figure:
1) selection of the appropriate blocks
2) noting whether or not the figure has rotational symmetry
3) noting the number of lines of mirror symmetry.

PATTERN LETTERS (Pages 99 — 105)

All these letters can be made with the pattern blocks.

FOOTBALL PATTERNS (Page 106)

Be sure that the student realizes that the area value for each piece represent the score from playing the piece and that the number of extra points cannot exceed the number of touchdowns.

PLACE VALUE (Pages 107 — 113)

Be sure the child uses only:
1 of each shape on page 107
2 of each shape on page 109
3 of each shape on page 111
5 of each shape on page 113

AREA AND PERIMETER (Pages 115 — 119)

This section provides concrete experience with area and perimeter. The tasks ask children to work with areas that remain the same while the perimeter changes, and with perimeters that remain the same while the area changes. Pages 119 and 120 ask the child to create their own shapes with specific areas and perimeters.

SQUARE, TRIANGULAR, HEXAGONAL NUMBERS (Pages 120 — 124)

Page 120 should be used as a recording sheet for questions on pages 121 and 124. After they complete the recording for the square and triangle, they should be able to build the sequence of patterns for each of the remaining pattern block shapes.

FRACTIONS (Pages 125 — 161)

Pages 125 — 127 introduce the concept of a unit fraction. Be sure the child writes the correct fraction in each region.

For initial success on the fraction coloring, pages 128 — 137, be sure the child correctly covers the shape before coloring. As long as is necessary, the teacher should check the way the shape is covered before the child colors.

Pages 138 — 143 require the child to complete a matrix. The answer key shows what is expected for these pages.

Pages 144 — 145 introduce the concept of a reciprocal. Be sure answers are recorded in fraction form, not as a mixed numeral. For example: the reciprocal of

$$\frac{2}{3} \quad \text{must be} \quad \frac{3}{2} \quad \text{not} \quad 1\frac{1}{2}$$

Pages 146 — 155 are reciprocal matrices. Answers should be written in fraction form.

Pages 156 — 160 provide opportunities for children to create their own fractions.

SET THEORY FRACTIONS (Pages 163 — 167)

These pages provide an extended experience with fractions coupled with some set theory logic.

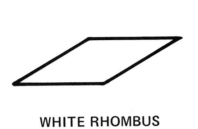

WHITE RHOMBUS

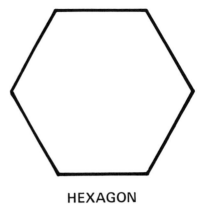

HEXAGON

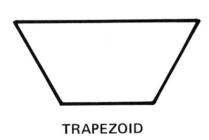

TRAPEZOID

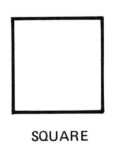

SQUARE

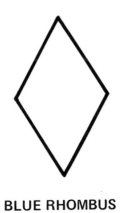

BLUE RHOMBUS

TRIANGLE

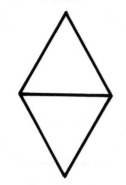

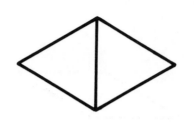

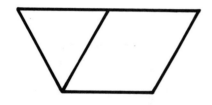

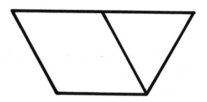

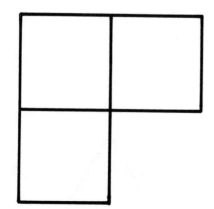

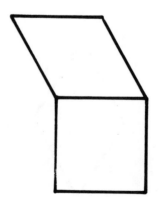

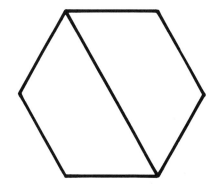

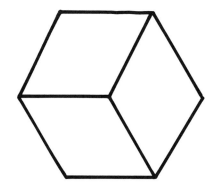

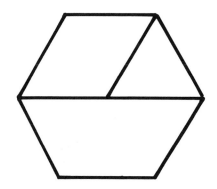

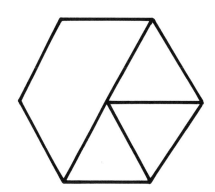

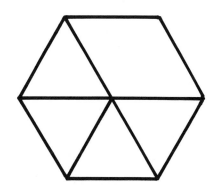

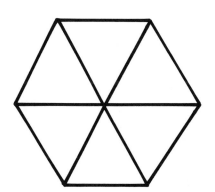

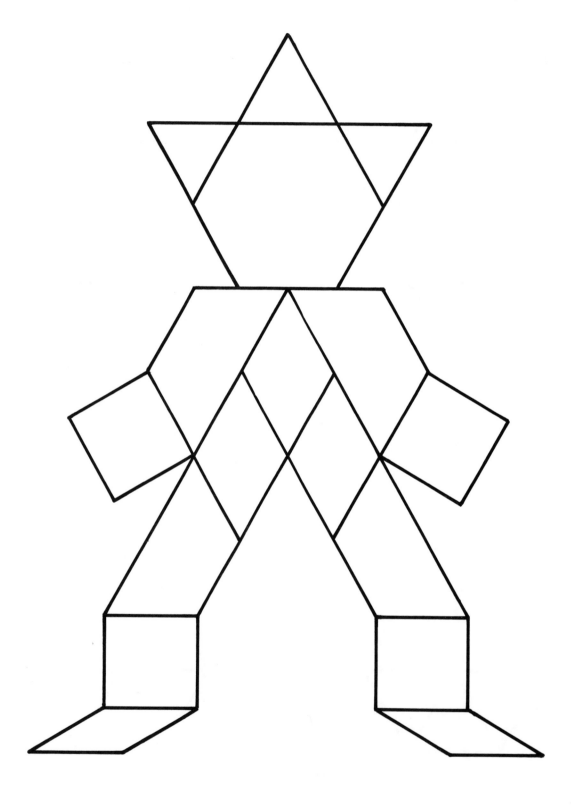

COVER EACH SHAPE WITH 3 BLOCKS.

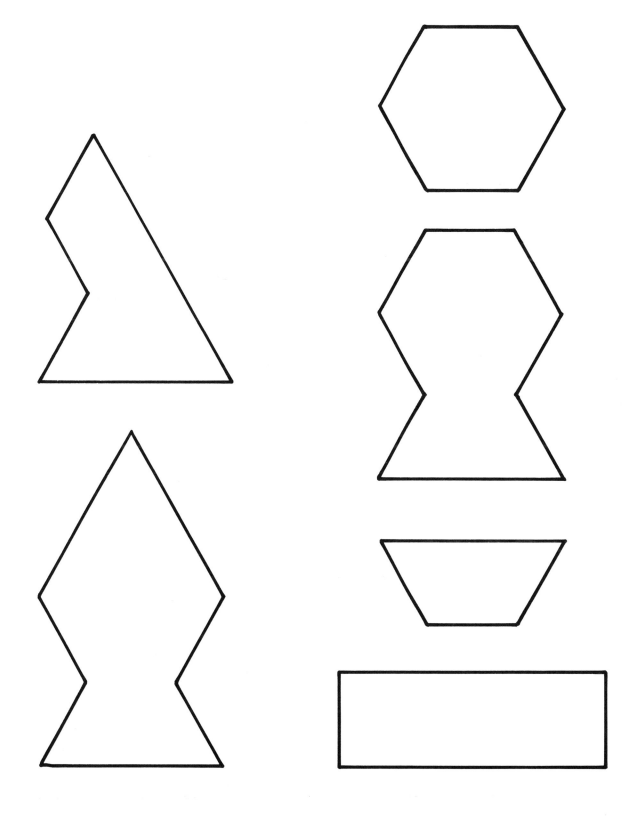

COVER WITH 4 PATTERN BLOCKS.

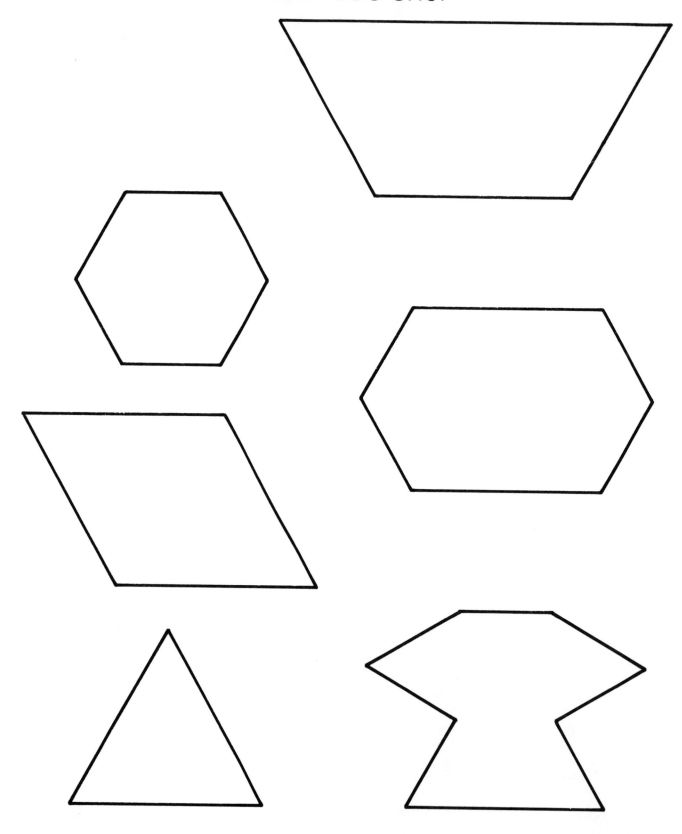

COVER WITH 5 PATTERN BLOCKS.

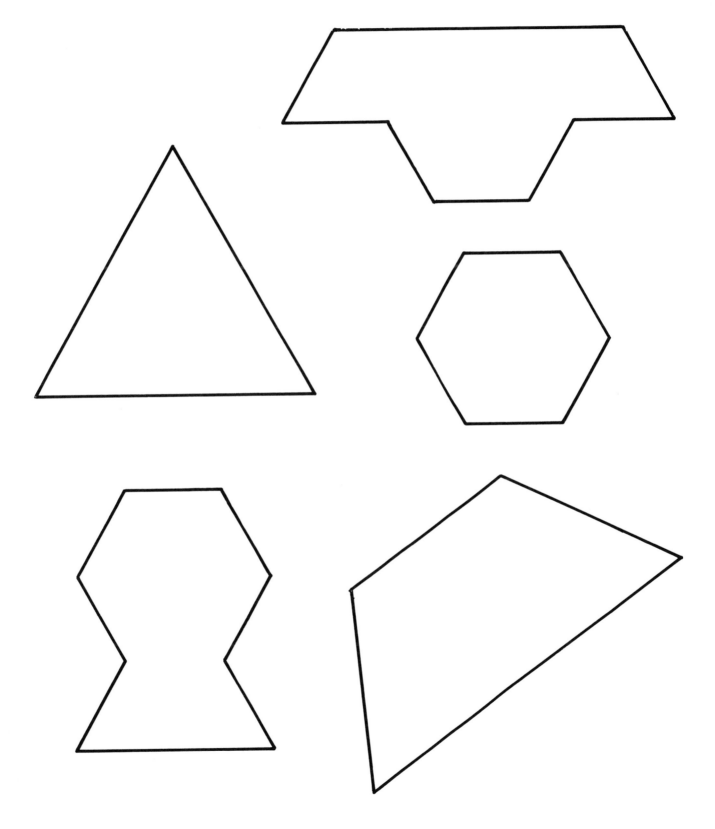

COVER WITH 6 PATTERN BLOCKS.

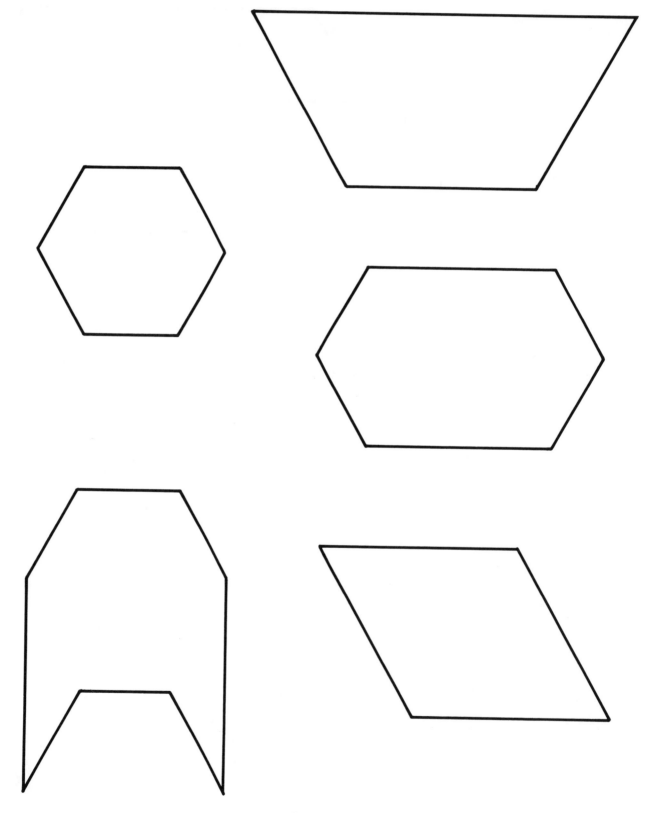

FOLLOW THE LEADER

AN ACTIVITY FOR THREE OR MORE PLAYERS.

THE FIRST PLAYER (NOW THE LEADER) SELECTS ANY PATTERN BLOCK SHAPE AND PLACES THAT SHAPE IN FRONT OF HIM IN A CERTAIN POSITION. EACH OF THE REMAINING PLAYERS SELECT THE SAME BLOCK AND PUT IT IN THE CORRECT POSITION. (SEE BELOW).

THE NEXT PLAYER (NOW THE LEADER) SELECTS A BLOCK OF HIS CHOICE AND PLACES IT INTO THE POSITION HE DESIRES AND EACH OF THE REMAINING PLAYERS DO THE SAME. (SEE BELOW).

THE ACTIVITY CONTINUES AROUND THE GROUP WITH EACH PLAYER TAKING TURNS BEING THE LEADER. ALL PLAYERS WILL END UP WITH THE SAME DESIGN OR PICTURE IF THEY CORRECTLY FOLLOWED THE LEADERS.

LEADER 1st PLAY

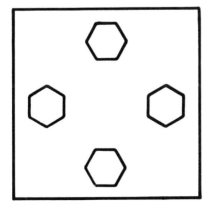

LEADER 2nd PLAY

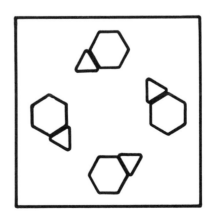

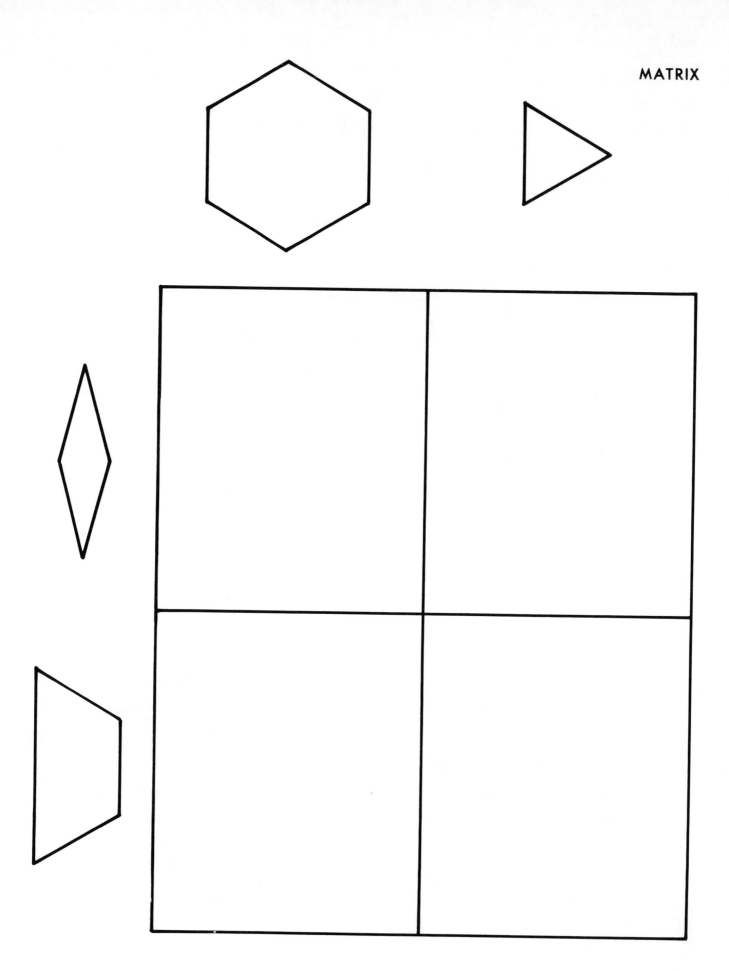

10

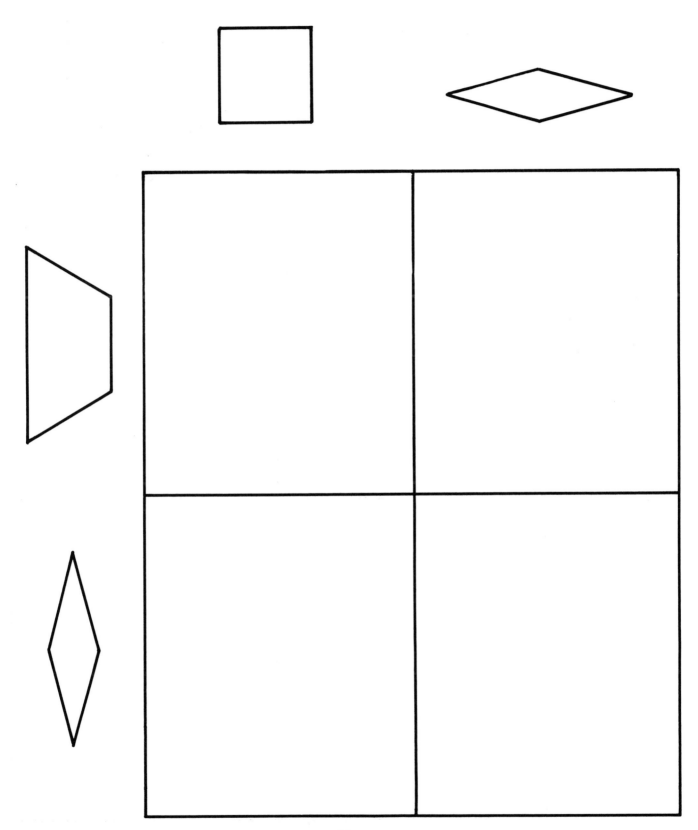

11

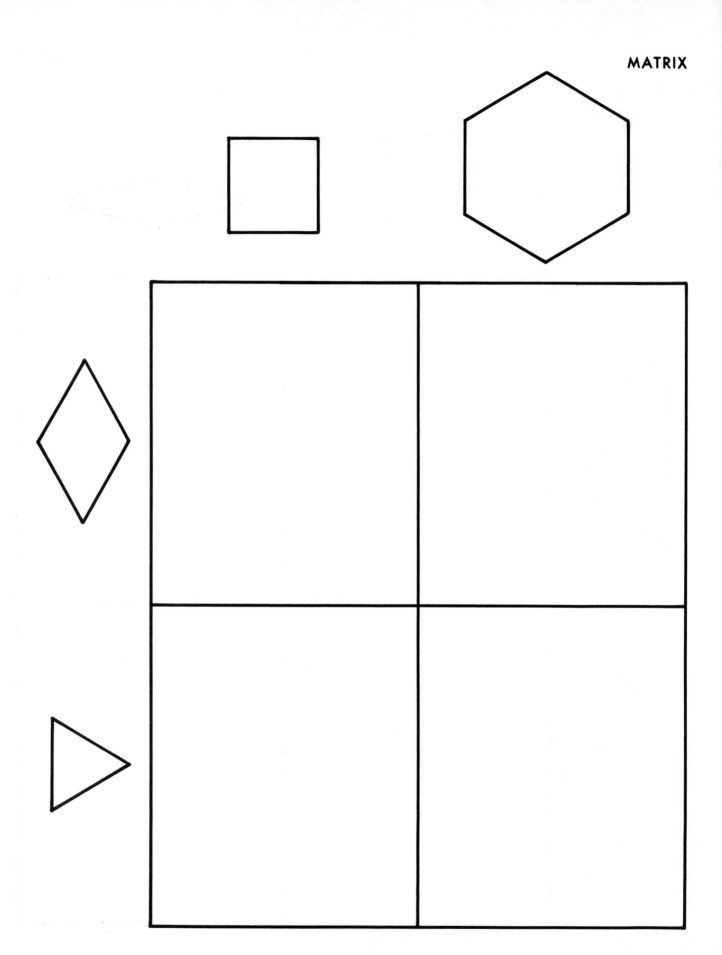

12

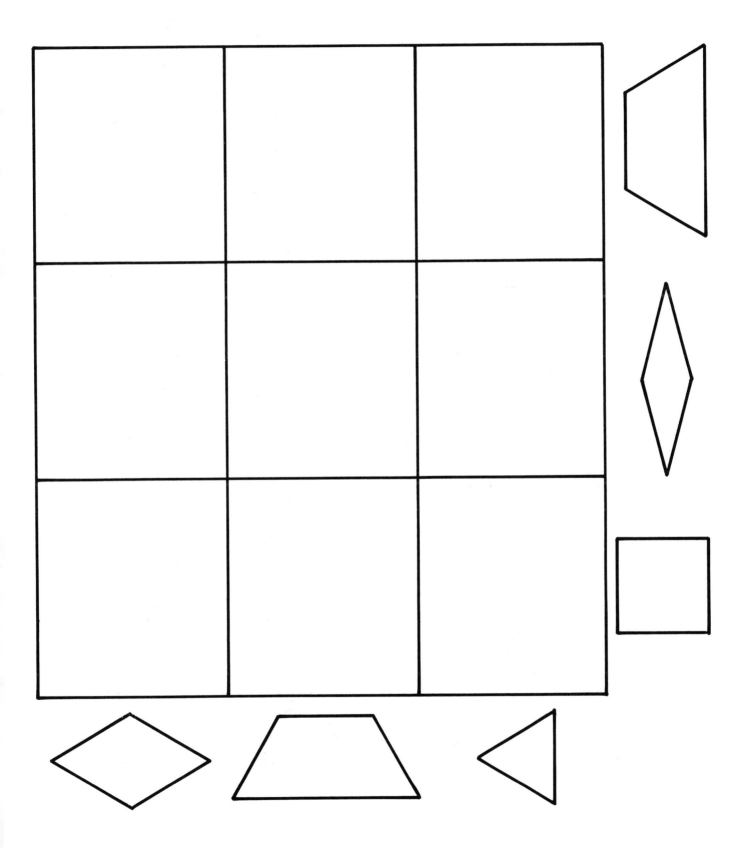

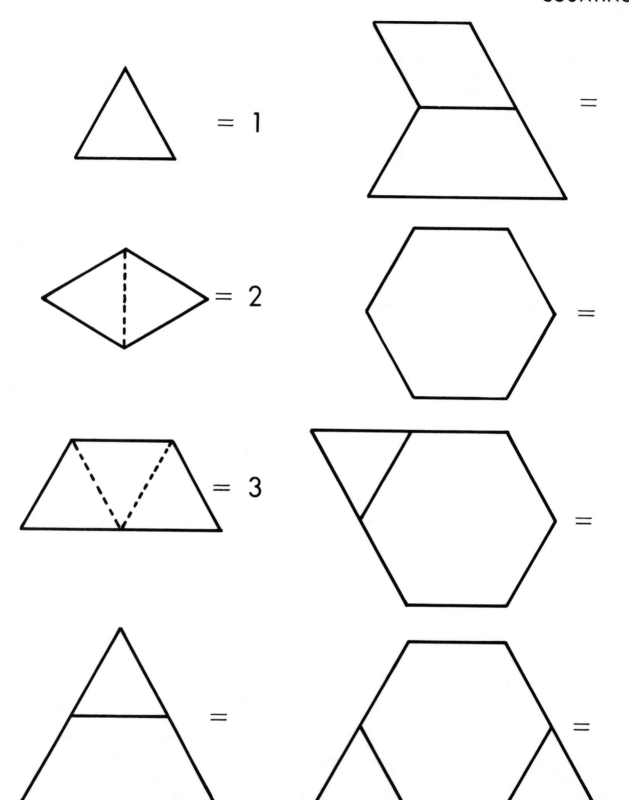

= 1

= 2

= 3

=

=

=

=

=

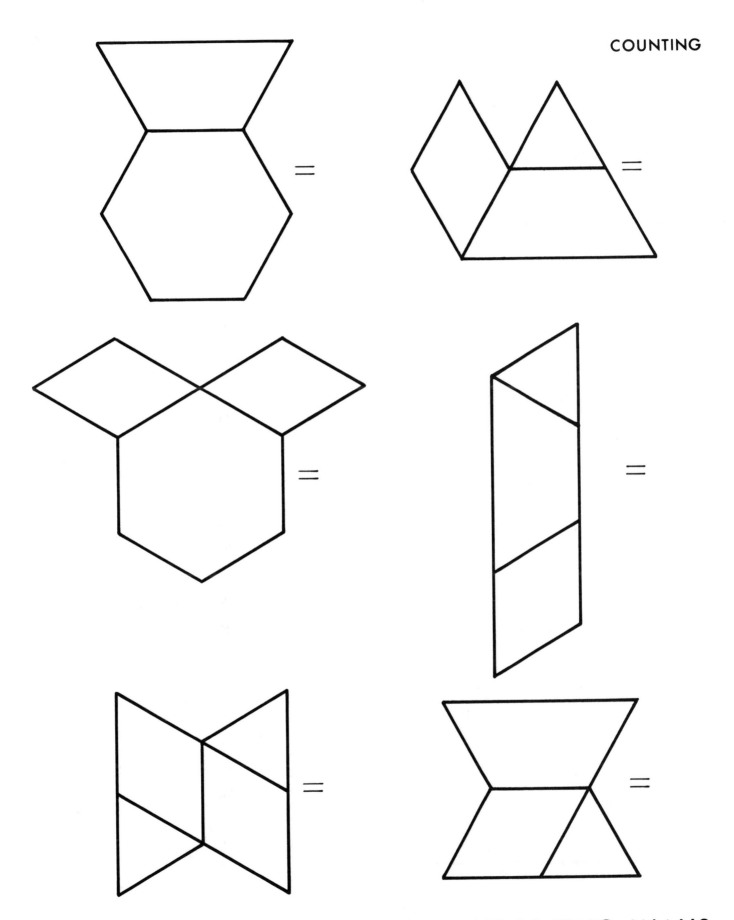

ON THE BACK OF THIS PAGE MAKE 10 TWO WAYS

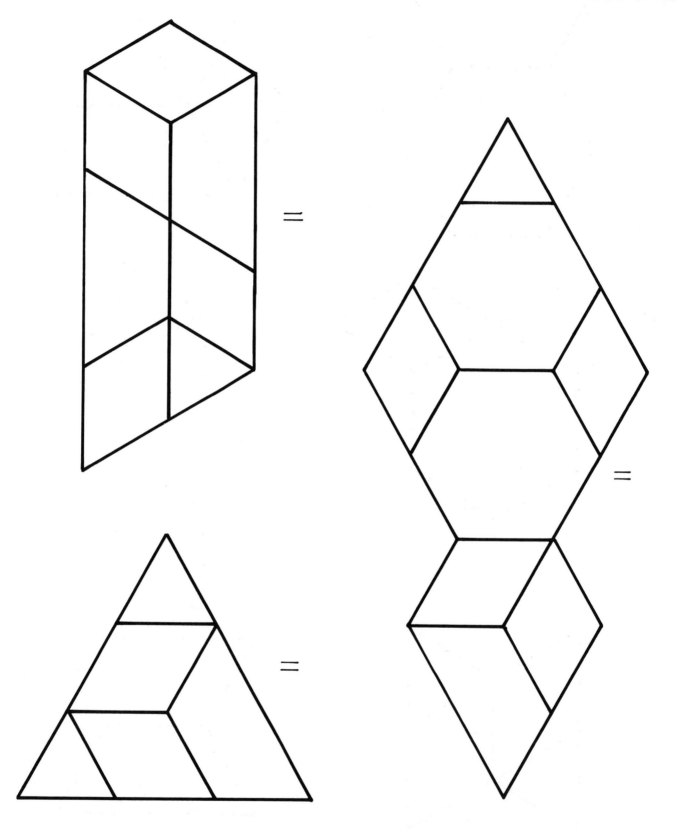

16

CAT STRATEGY

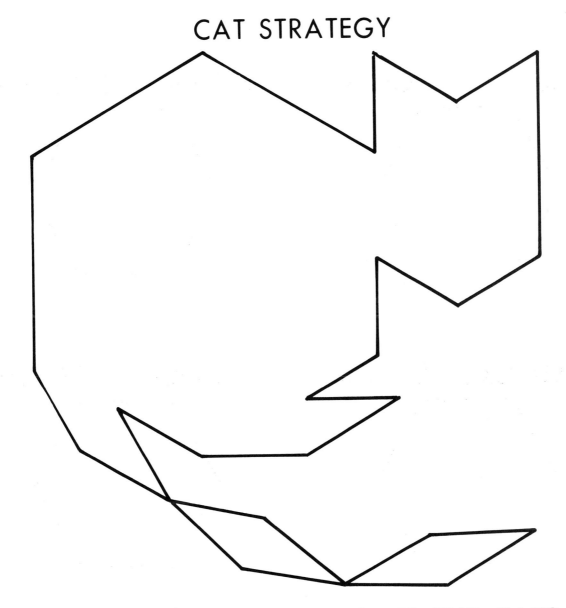

HOW MANY BLOCKS COVER THE CAT?

1	2	3	4	5	6	7	8	9	10
11	12	13	14	15	16	17	18	19	20
21	22	23	24	25	26	27	28	29	30
31	32	33	34	35	36	37	38	39	40

2 BLOCKS 1 COLOR

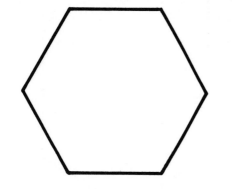

3 BLOCKS 3 COLORS

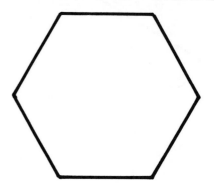

3 BLOCKS 1 COLOR

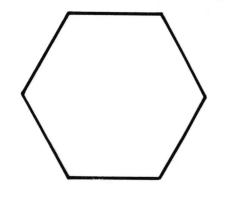

5 BLOCKS 2 COLORS

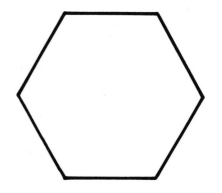

6 BLOCKS 1 COLOR

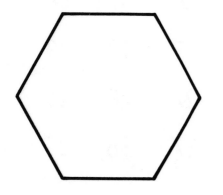

4 BLOCKS 2 COLORS

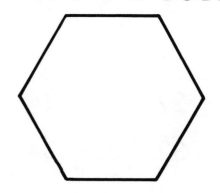

4 BLOCKS 2 COLORS

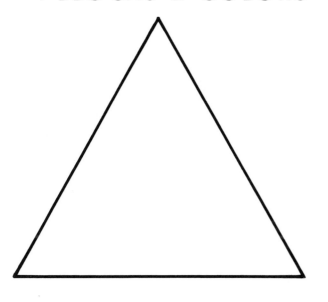

3 BLOCKS 1 COLOR

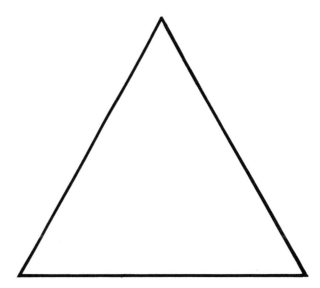

5 BLOCKS 3 COLORS

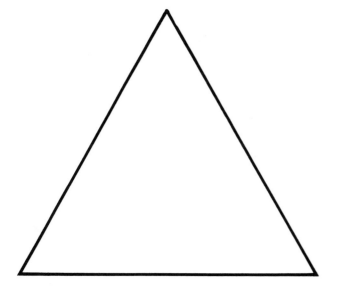

6 BLOCKS 2 COLORS

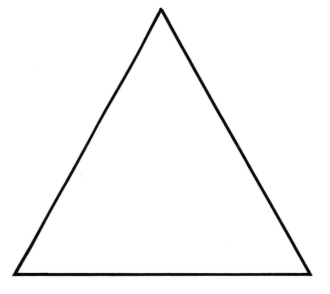

4 BLOCKS 1 COLOR

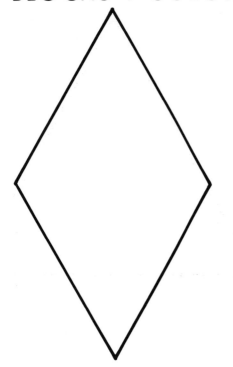

4 BLOCKS 3 COLORS

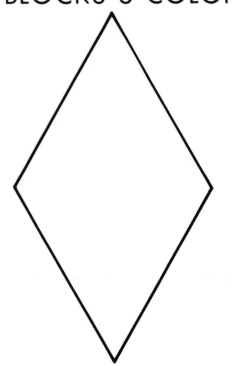

3 BLOCKS 2 COLORS

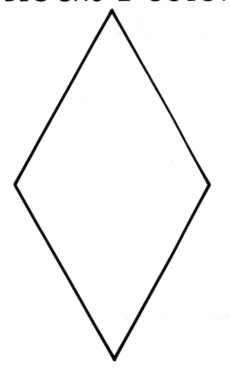

6 BLOCKS 2 COLORS

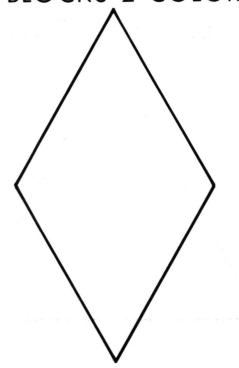

4 BLOCKS 1 COLOR

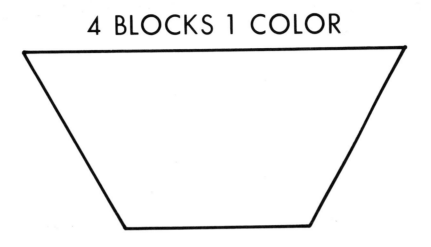

5 BLOCKS 3 COLORS

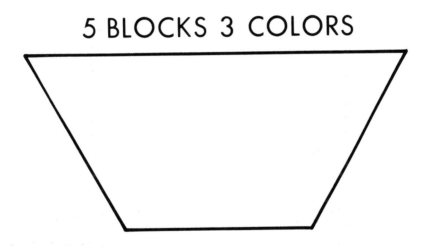

6 BLOCKS 3 COLORS

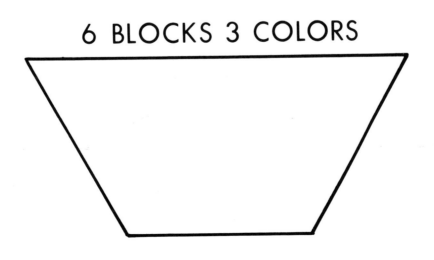

4 BLOCKS 2 COLORS

4 BLOCKS 3 COLORS

5 BLOCKS 4 COLORS

6 BLOCKS 3 COLORS

8 BLOCKS 2 COLORS

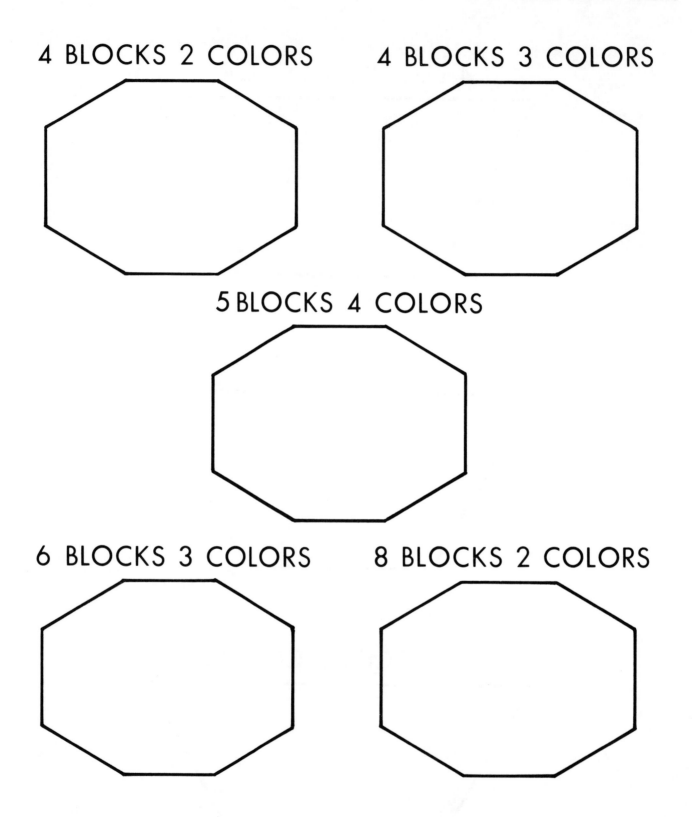

2 COLORS 4 BLOCKS

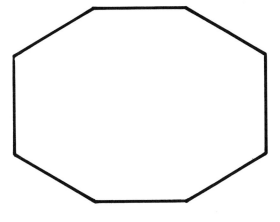

3 COLORS 4 BLOCKS

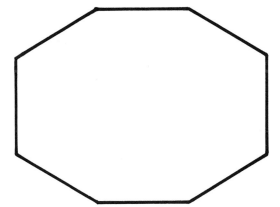

4 COLORS 5 BLOCKS

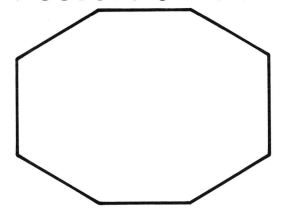

3 COLORS 6 BLOCKS

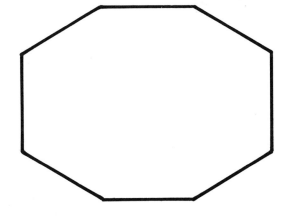

4 BLOCKS 2 COLORS

6 BLOCKS 4 COLORS

6 BLOCKS 2 COLORS

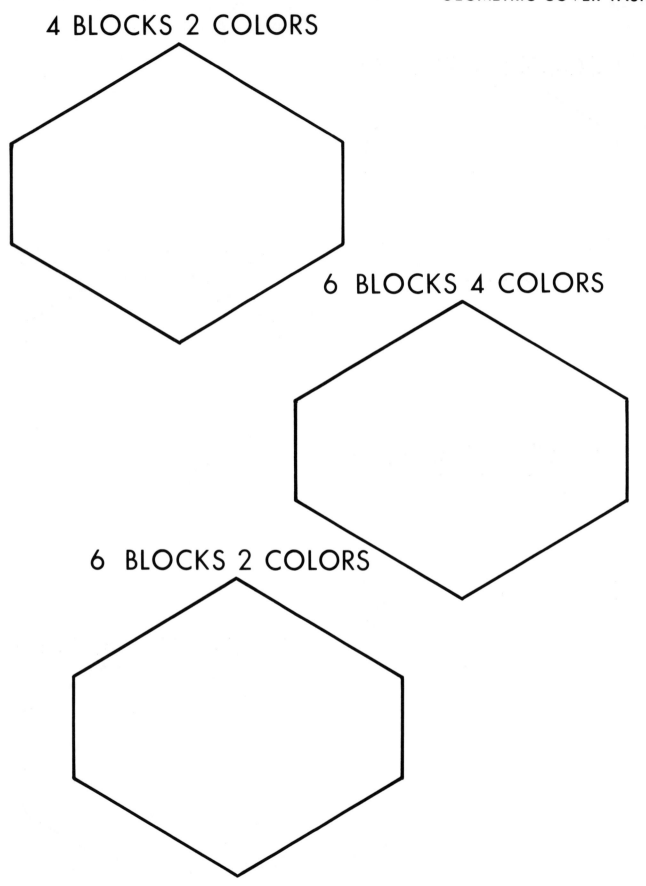

7 BLOCKS 2 COLORS

6 BLOCKS 2 COLORS

10 BLOCKS

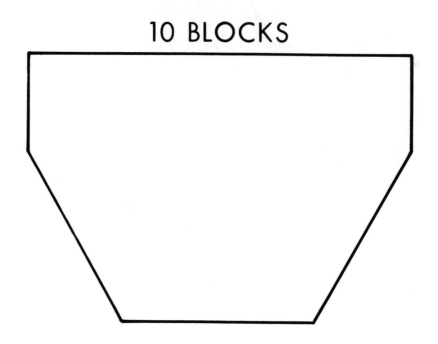

9 BLOCKS 3 COLORS

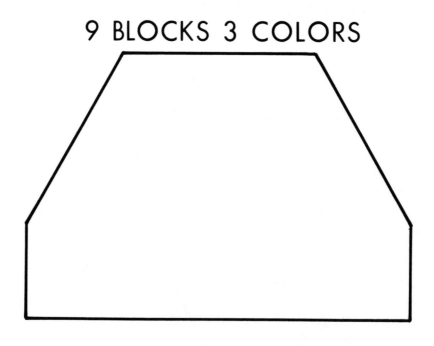

2 COLORS 7 BLOCKS

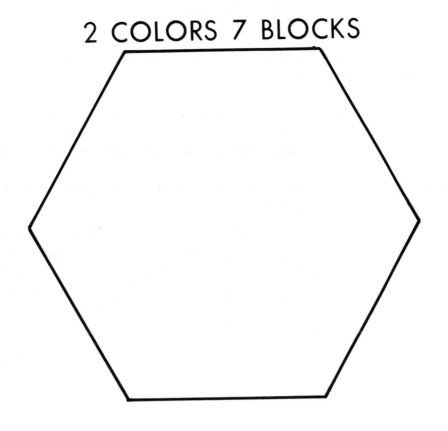

3 COLORS 13 BLOCKS

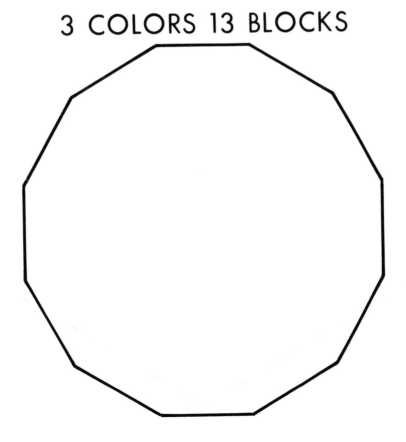

LAST BLOCK

An activity for two or more players. The playing surface is the hexagon below. Use only Green, Blue, Red and Yellow pieces.

Play begins with a green triangle placed at the top of the hexagon as shown below. Each player takes turns placing any pattern block of his choice on the playing surface such that at least one complete side is touching a pattern block already on the playing surface.

THE WINNER IS THE PLAYER WHO PLACES THE LAST BLOCK THAT COMPLETELY FILLS THE HEXAGON.

Or you could change
the rule so that the
player placing the last
block is the loser.

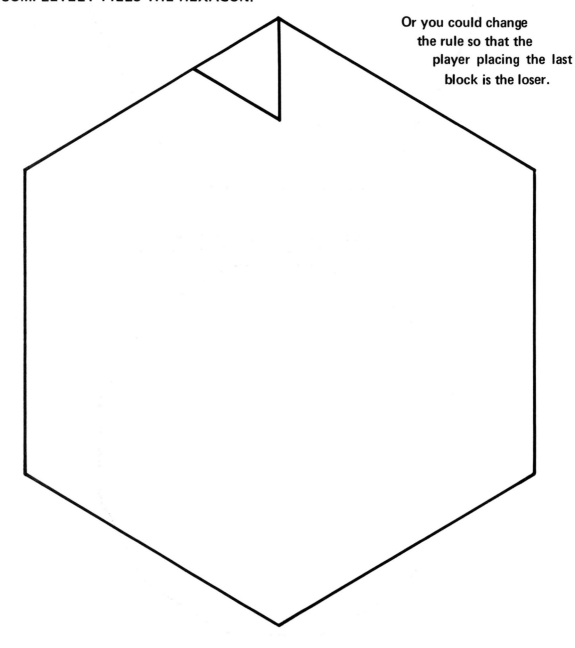

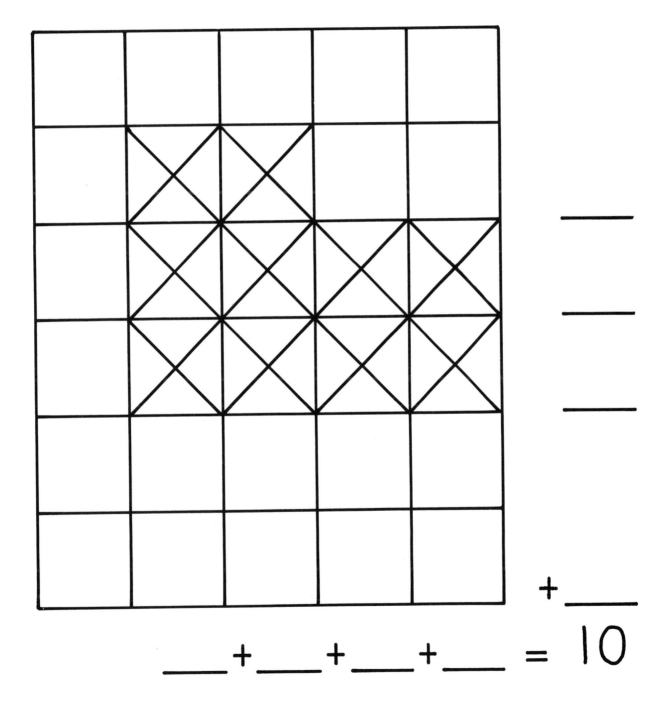

___

___

___

$+$___

___$+$___$+$___$+$___ $= 10$

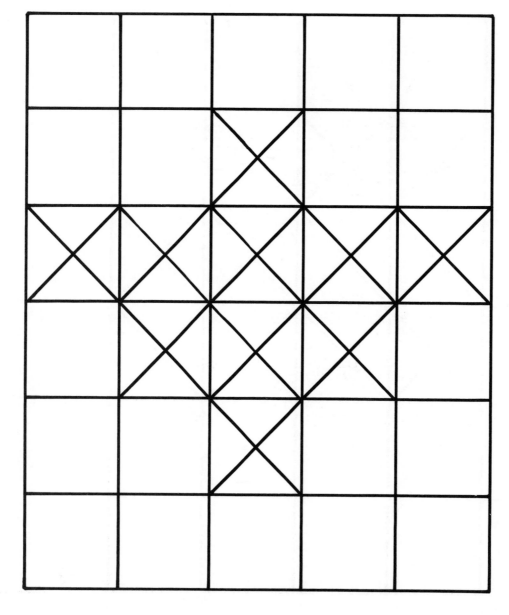

$+$ _____
$=$ 10

$$+\underline{}$$
$$=10$$

BLOCK-IT

EACH PLAYER RECEIVES THREE BLOCKS EACH OF THE FOLLOWING COLORS (Green, Blue, Red, and Yellow).

POINT VALUE OF EACH COLOR

GREEN = 1   BLUE = 2   RED = 3   YELLOW = 6

THE GAME BEGINS WITH ONE YELLOW HEXAGON PLACED ON THE PLAYING SURFACE.

THE FIRST PLAYER MUST PLACE ANY OF HIS BLOCKS SUCH THAT ONE SIDE OF HIS BLOCK IS COMPLETELY TOUCHING ON ONE SIDE OF THE YELLOW BLOCK. THE SCORING FOR EACH PLAY IS THE SUM OF THE VALUES FOR THE BLOCKS THAT ARE TOUCHING THE BLOCKS PLAYED.

1st Play • Player "A" selected a green triangle to play, therefore yellow and green blocks are touching so points are scored.

6 + 1 = 7

Scoring Sheet Player A
1) 7
2) _____ _____

2nd Play • Player "B" selected a red trapezoid to play. Because it is touching one full side of the yellow hexagon and one full side of the green triangle the score is 10 points.

6 + 1 + 3 = 10

Scoring Sheet Player B
1) 10
2) _____ _____

3rd Play • Player "A" selected a blue rhombus to play. Scoring is 8 points since blue and yellow sides are touching.

6 + 2 = 8

Scoring Sheet Player A
1) 7
2) 8   15
3) _____ _____

4th Play • Player "B" selected a green triangle to play. Scoring is 6 points since 2 blocks are touching at least one complete side.

1 + 2 + 3 = 6

Scoring Sheet Player B
1) 10
2) 6   16

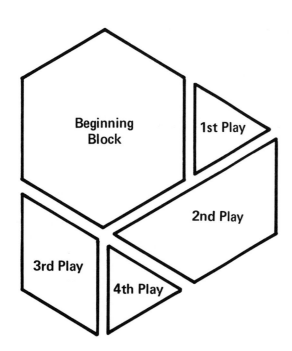

32

BLOCK-IT
SCORING SHEET

TOTAL

1) _____

2) _____   _____

3) _____   _____

4) _____   _____

5) _____   _____

6) _____   _____

7) _____   _____

8) _____   _____

9) _____   _____

10) _____   _____

11) _____   _____

12) _____   _____

GRAND TOTAL

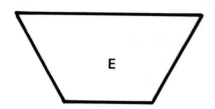

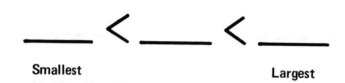

Smallest   Largest

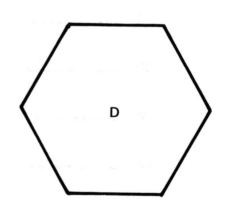

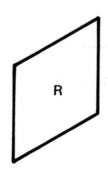

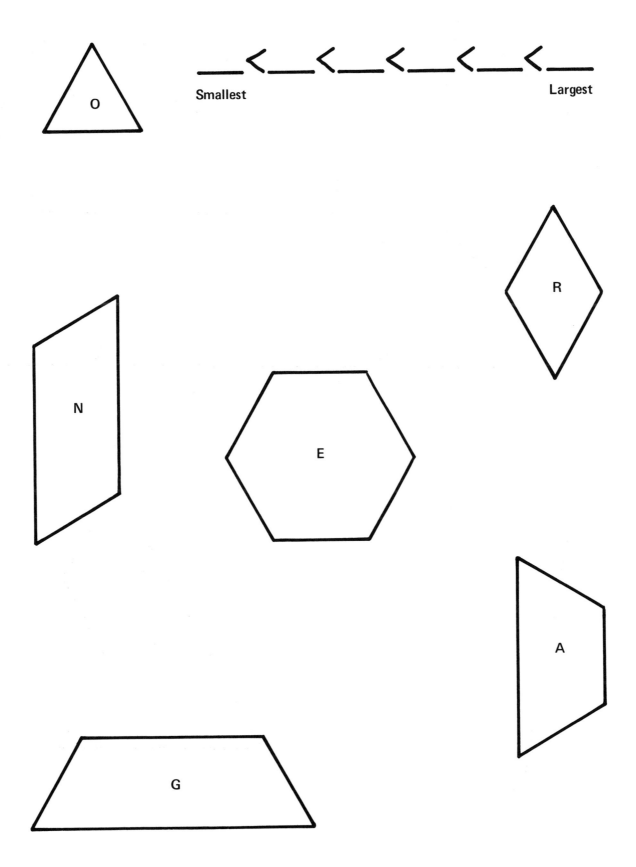

Smallest ___ < ___ < ___ < ___ < ___ Largest

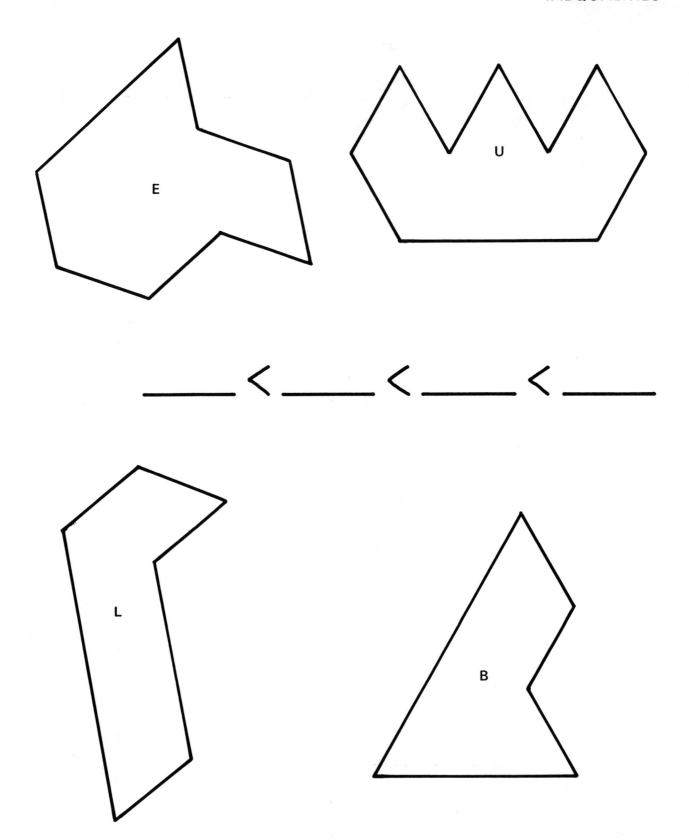

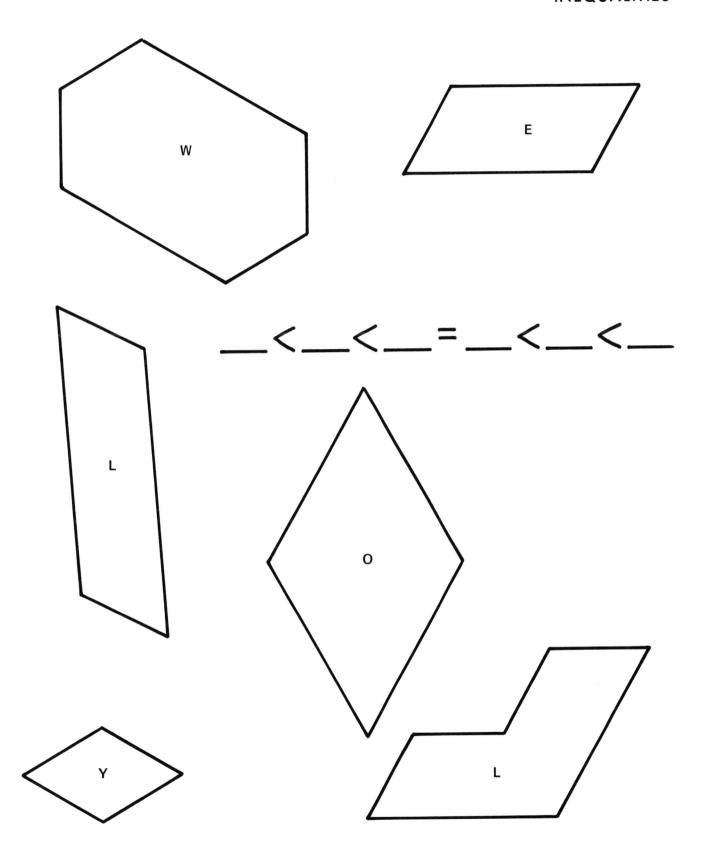

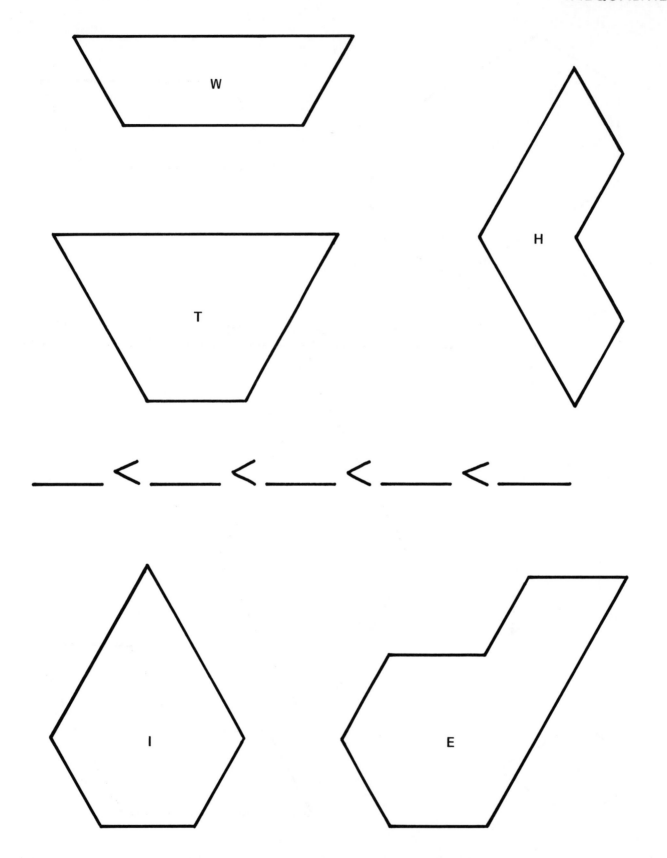

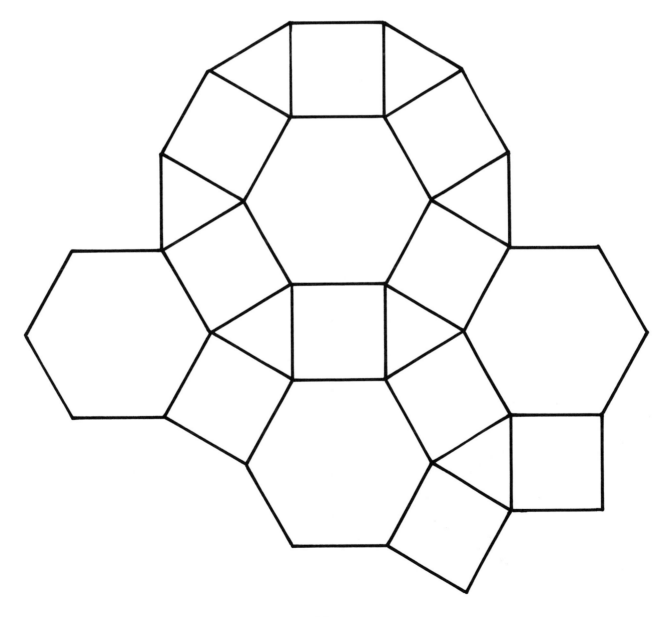

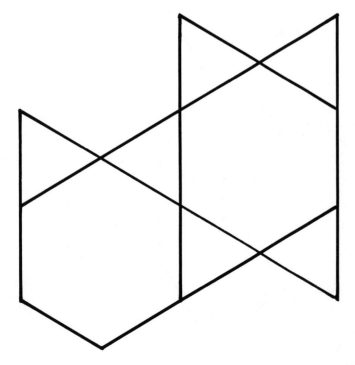

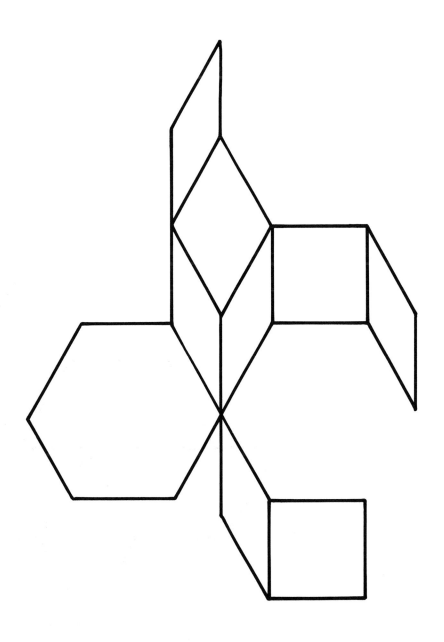

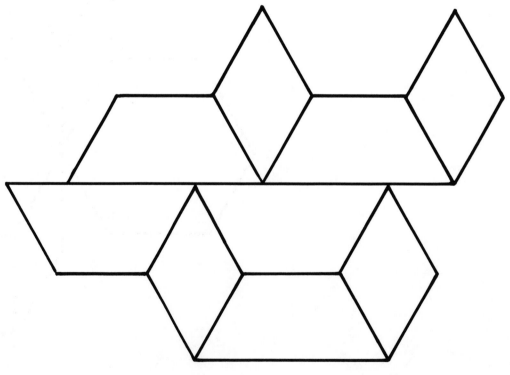

TREE

STRATEGY

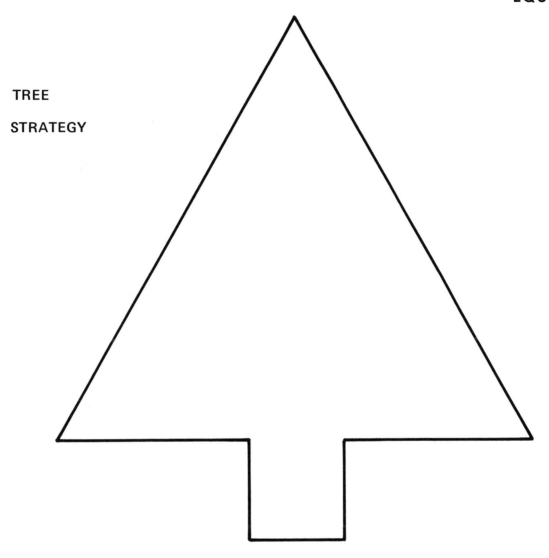

CIRCLE THE NUMBER OF BLOCKS THAT WILL COVER THE TREE.

1	2	3	4	5	6	7	8	9	10	11
12	13	14	15	16	17	18	19	20	21	22
23	24	25	26	27	28	29	30	31	32	33

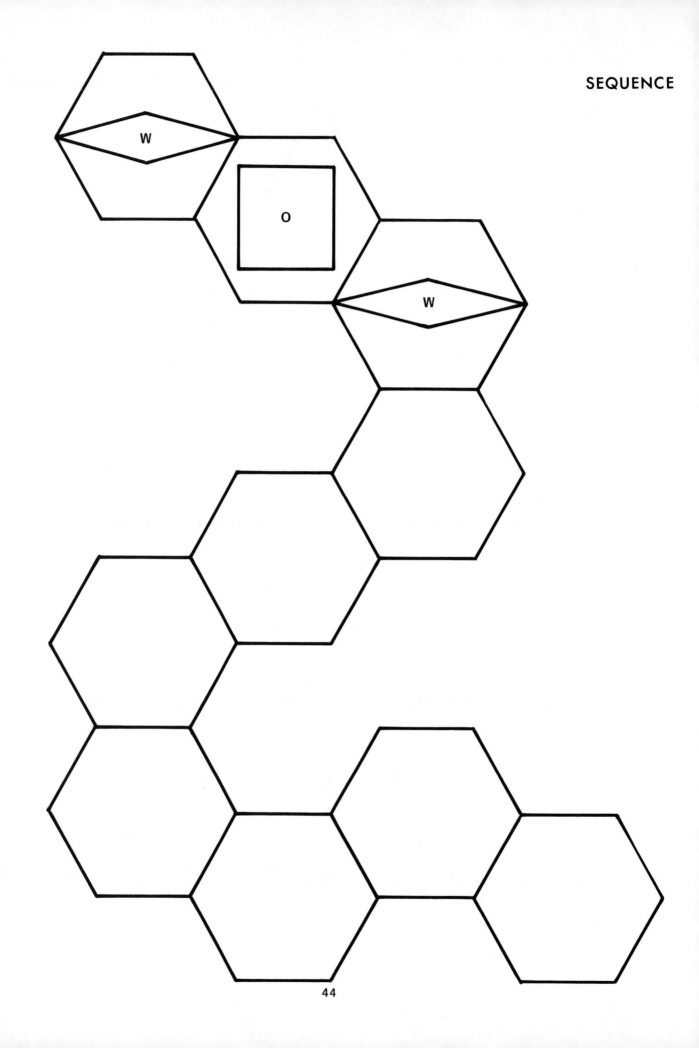

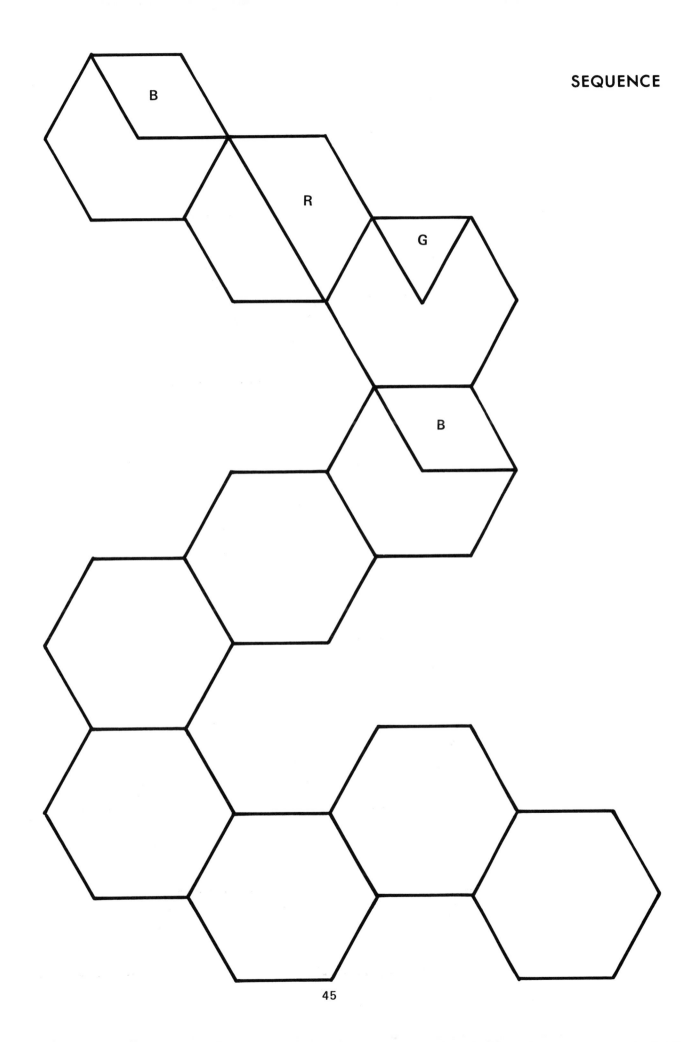

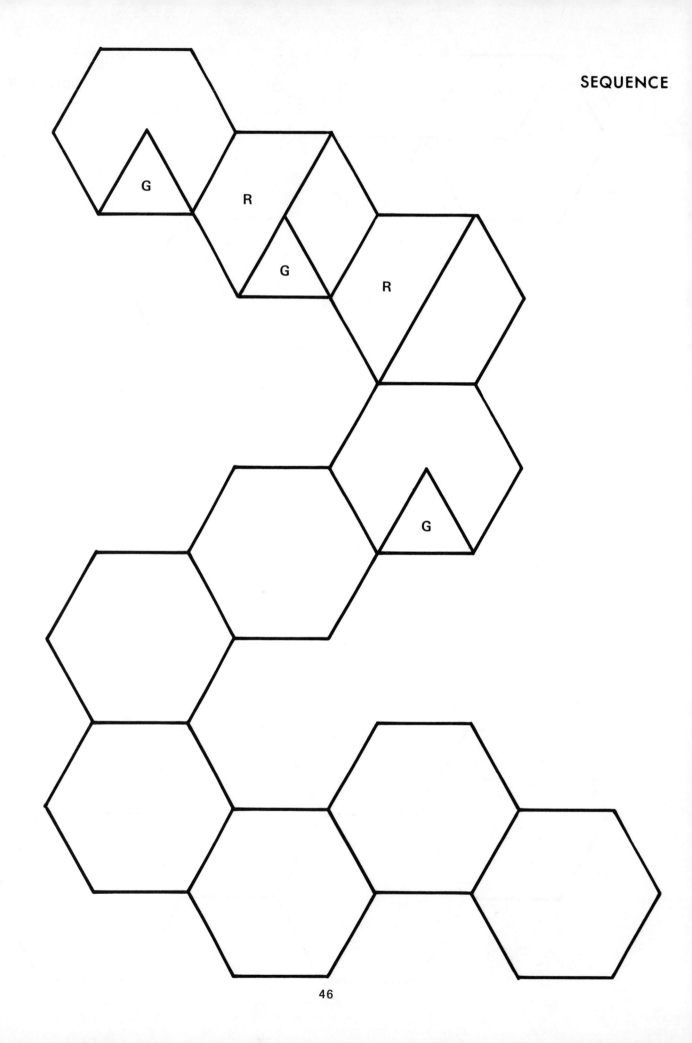

46

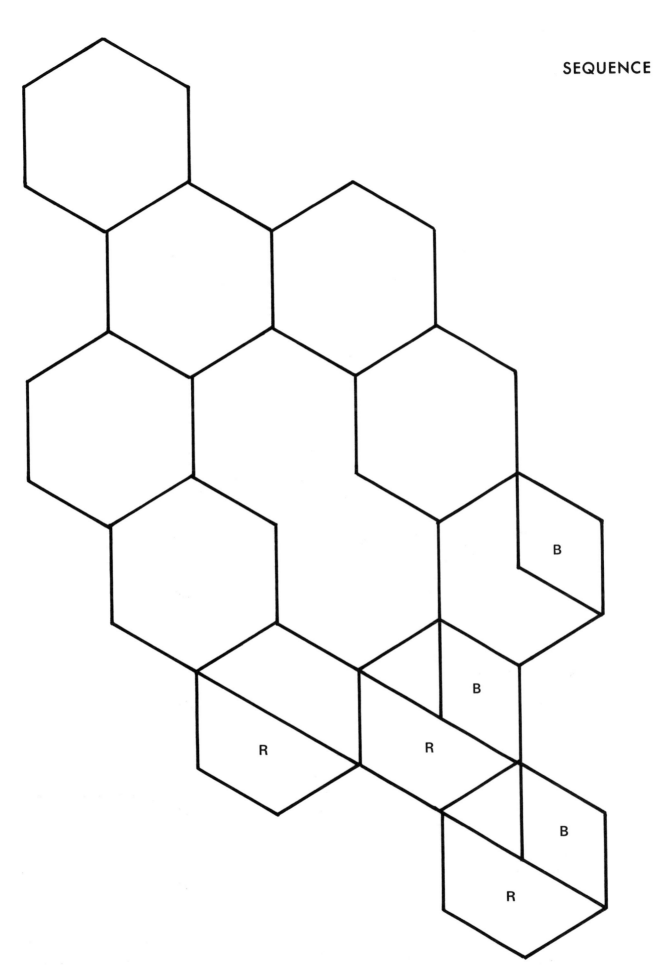

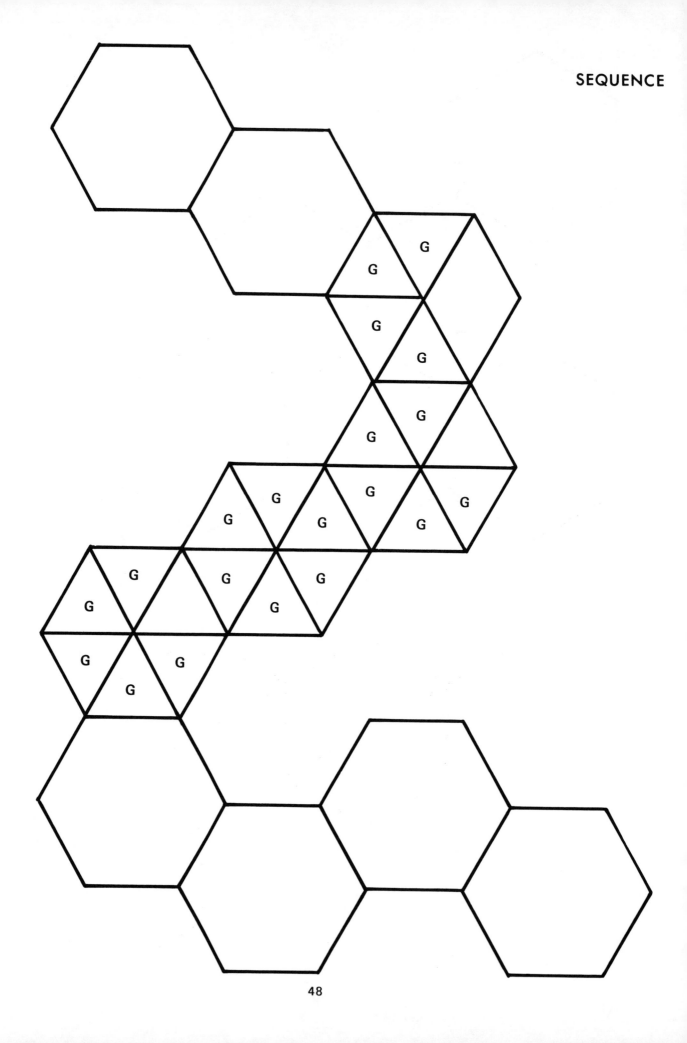

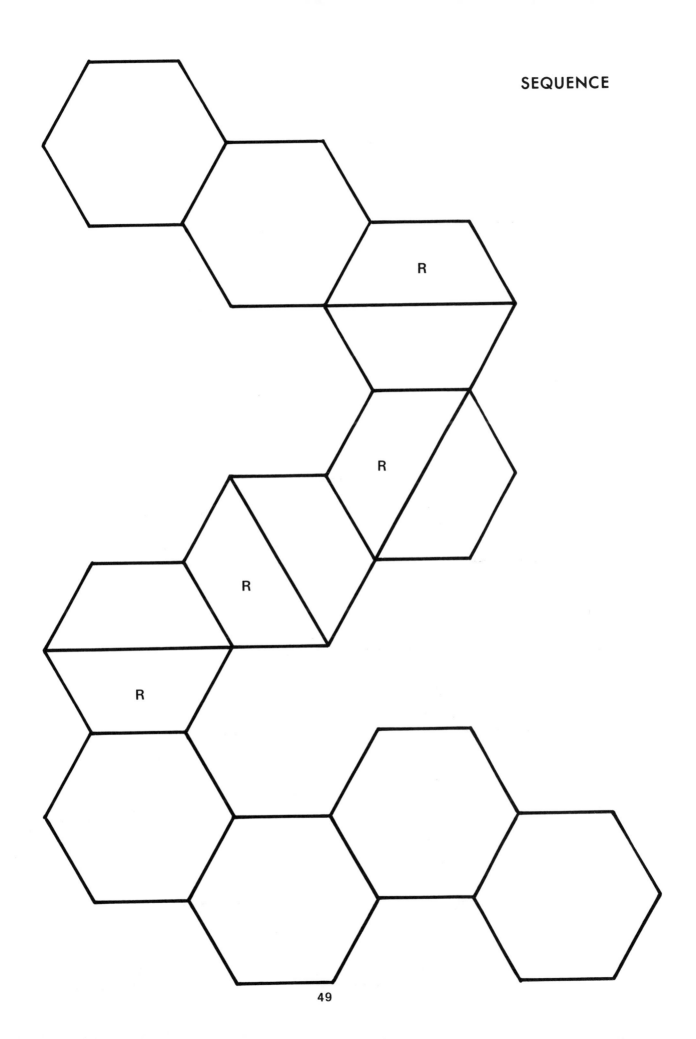

SEQUENCE

49

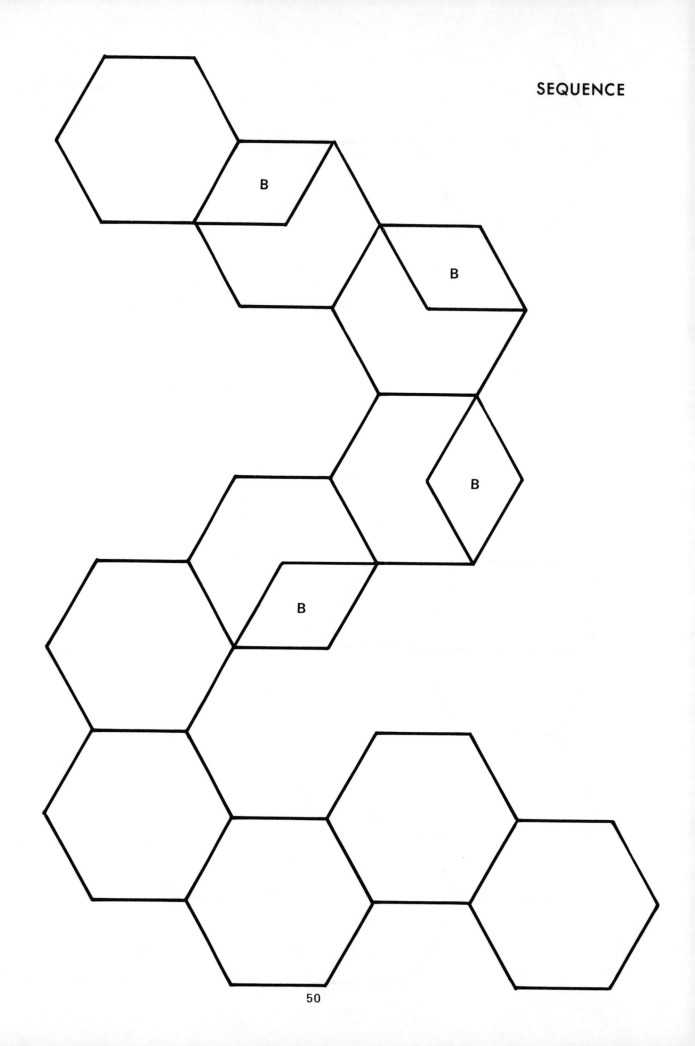

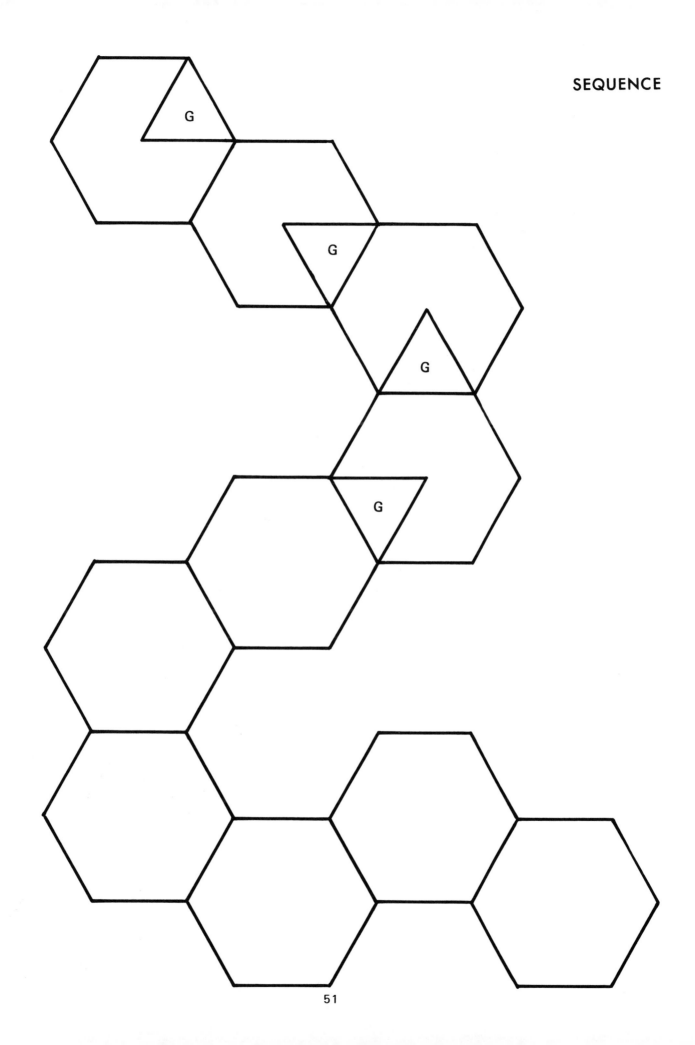

51

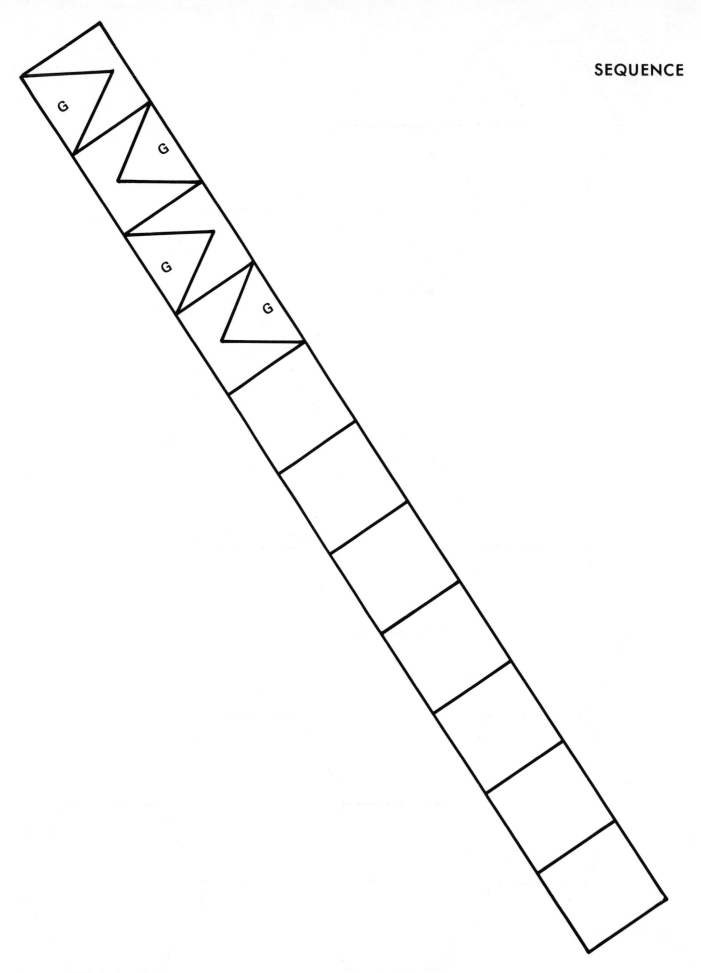

52

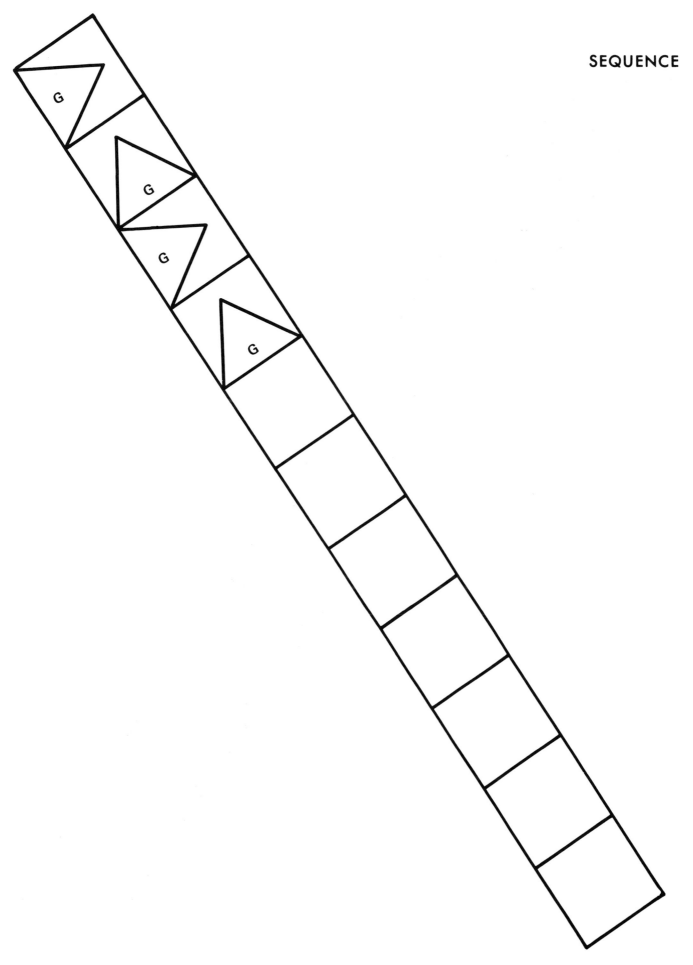

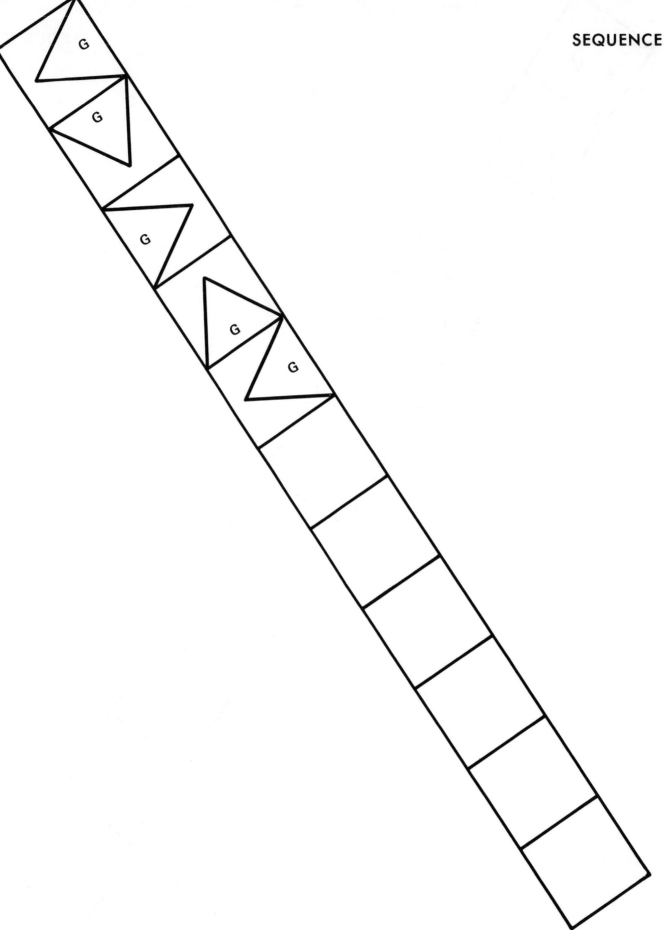

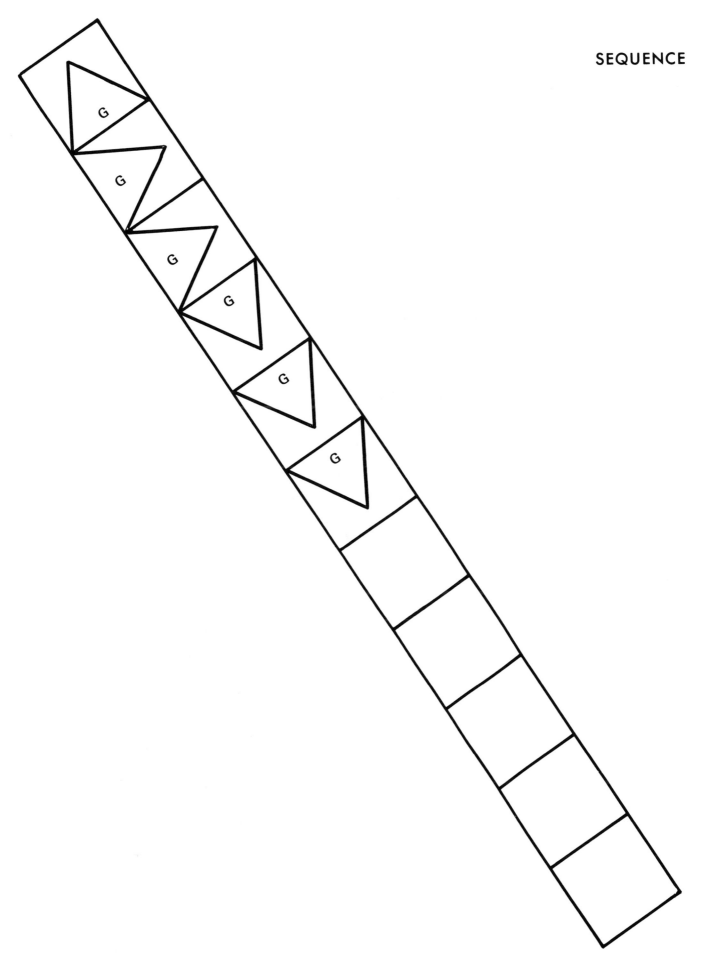

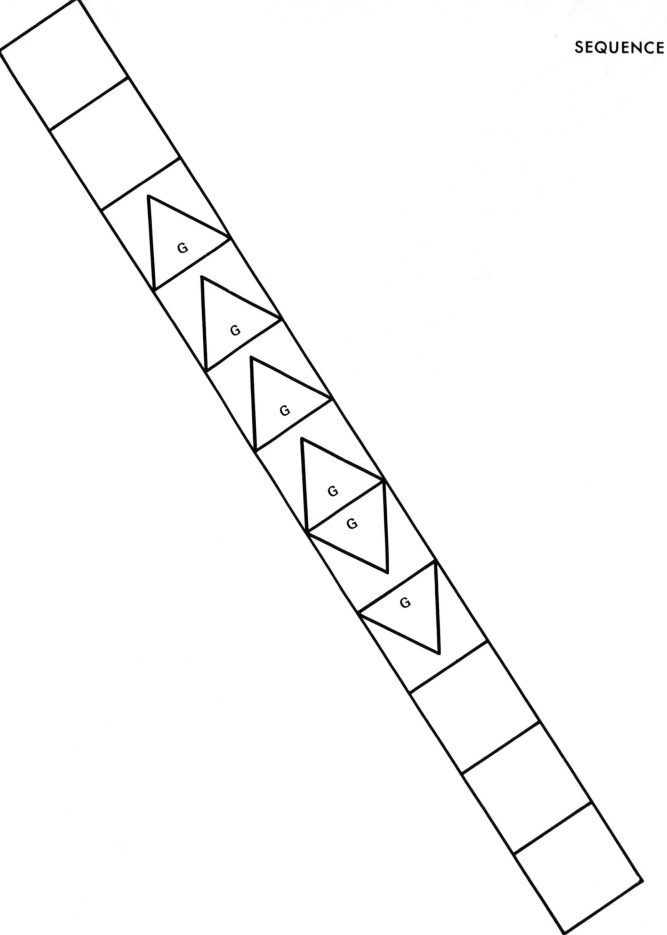

56

A. PICK UP THESE PIECES.

What numbers can you make using only these pieces?

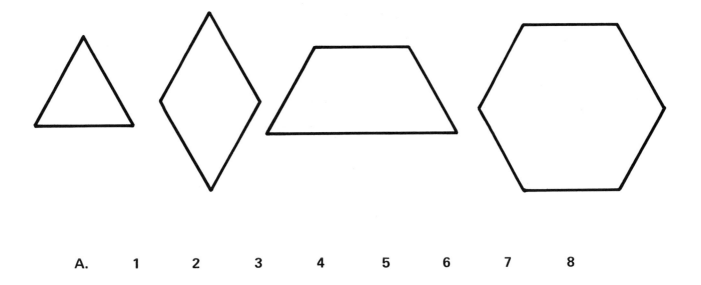

A.   1   2   3   4   5   6   7   8

9   10   11   12   13   14   15   16

B. PICK UP THESE PIECES?

What numbers can you make with these pieces?

B.   1   2   3   4   5   6

7   8   9   10   11   12

A. PICK UP THESE PIECES.

What numbers can you make with these pieces?

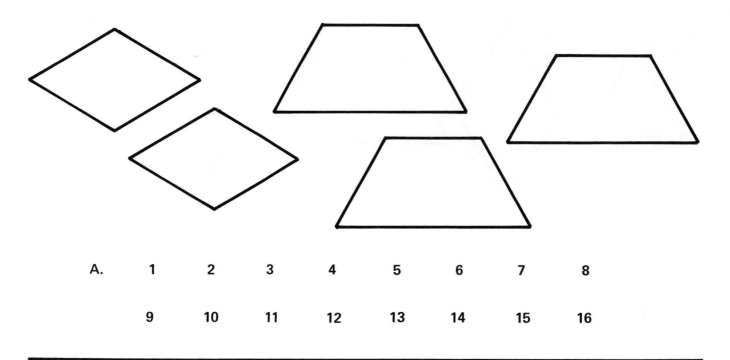

A.   1   2   3   4   5   6   7   8

       9   10   11   12   13   14   15   16

B. PICK UP THESE PIECES.

What numbers can you make with these pieces?

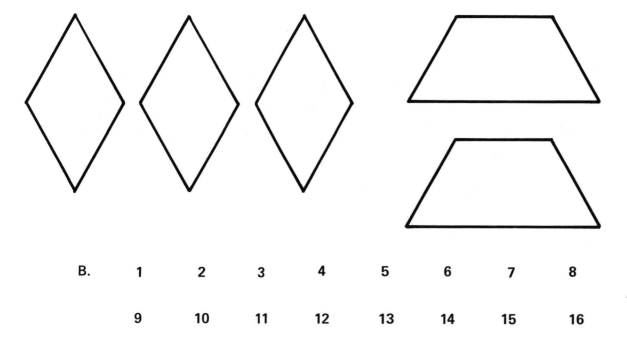

B.   1   2   3   4   5   6   7   8

       9   10   11   12   13   14   15   16

A. PICK UP THESE PIECES.

What numbers can you make with these pieces?

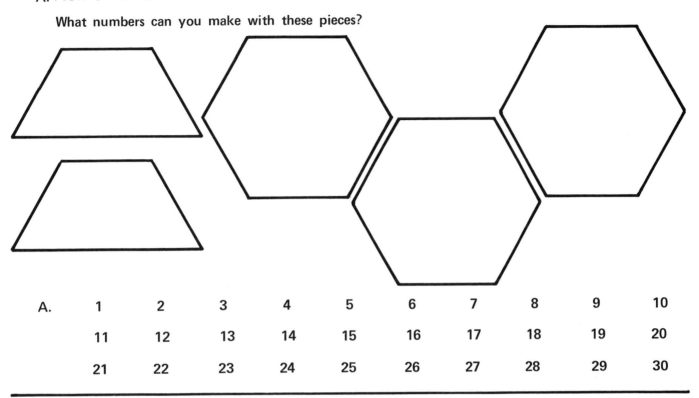

A.	1	2	3	4	5	6	7	8	9	10
	11	12	13	14	15	16	17	18	19	20
	21	22	23	24	25	26	27	28	29	30

B. PICK UP THESE PIECES.

What numbers can you make with these pieces?

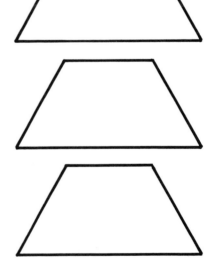

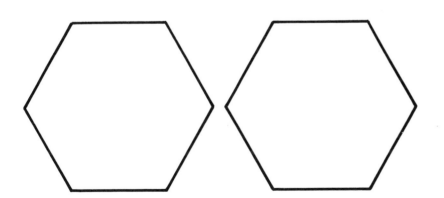

B.	1	2	3	4	5	6	7	8	9	10
	11	12	13	14	15	16	17	18	19	20
	21	22	23	24	25	26	27	28	29	30

DRAW TWO LINES TO EACH CLOCK.

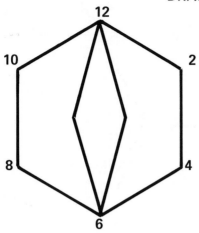

— 10 minutes to 4:00

— 12:30

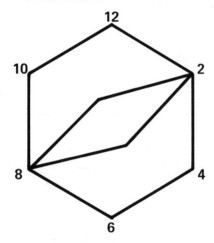

— 20 minutes after 10:00

— 20 minutes to 2:00

— 6:00

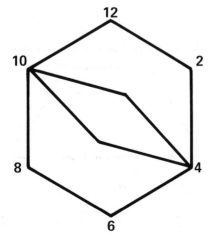

— 10 minutes after 8:00

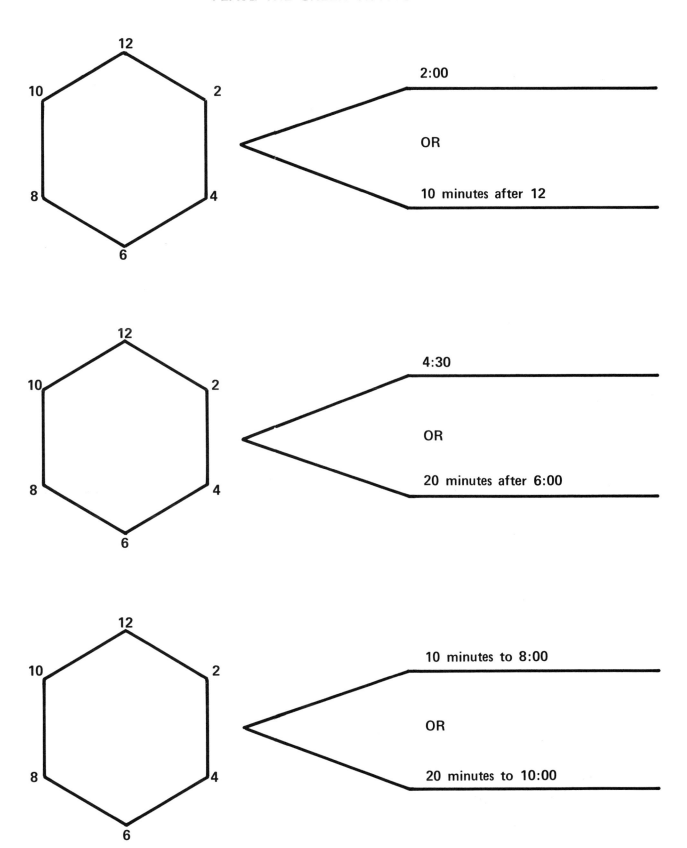

2:00

OR

10 minutes after 12

4:30

OR

20 minutes after 6:00

10 minutes to 8:00

OR

20 minutes to 10:00

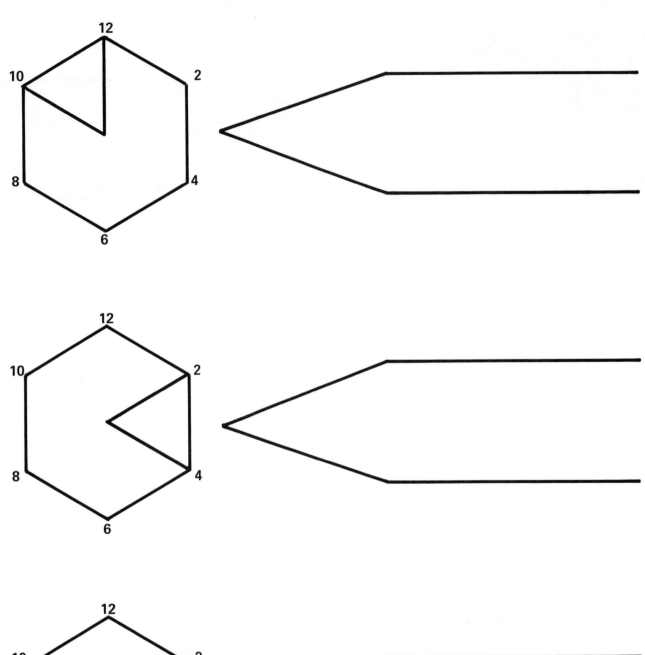

65

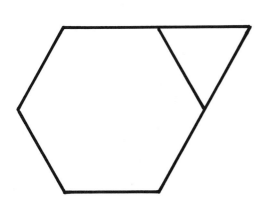
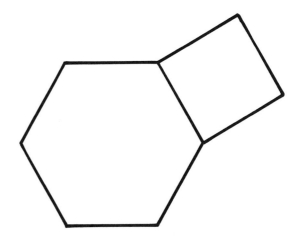

THESE ARE EGGYS.

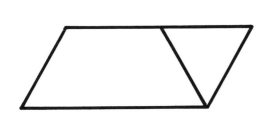
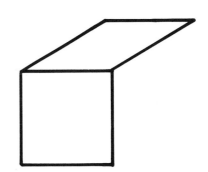

THESE ARE <u>NOT</u> EGGYS.

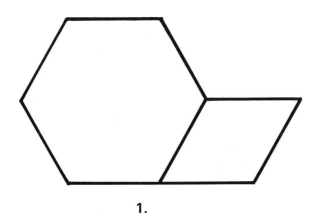

1.

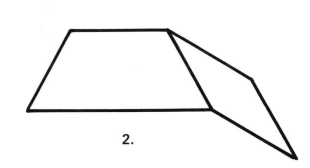

2.

CIRCLE THE EGGYS.

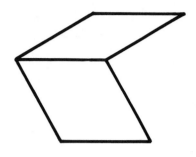

THESE ARE EELS.

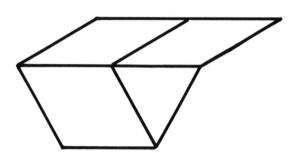
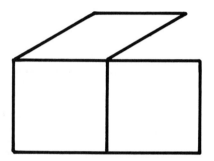

THESE ARE **NOT** EELS.

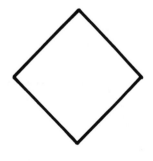
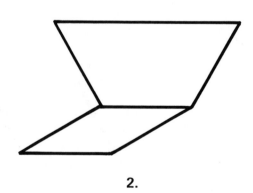

1.

2.

CIRCLE THE EELS.

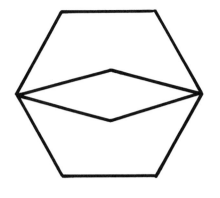

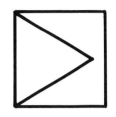

THESE ARE YANDS.

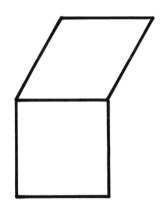

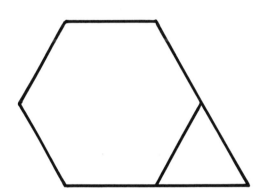

THESE ARE <u>NOT</u> YANDS.

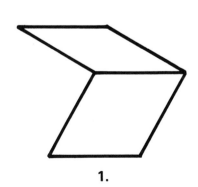

1.

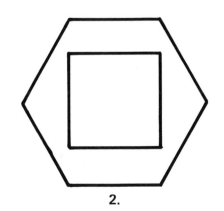

2.

CIRCLE THE YANDS.

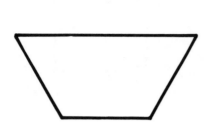
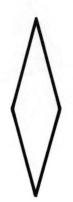

THESE ARE JEMS.

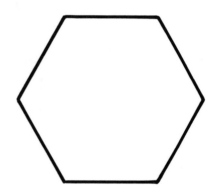

THESE ARE <u>NOT</u> JEMS.

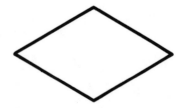

1.

2.

CIRCLE THE JEMS.

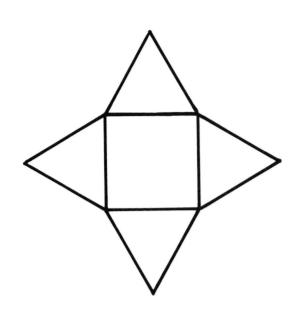

CLASSIFICATION

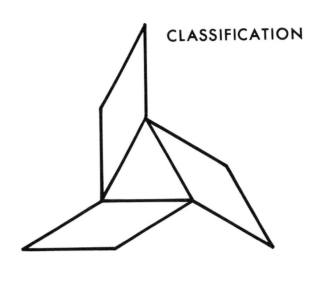

THESE ARE YACKS.

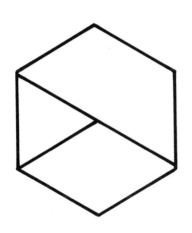

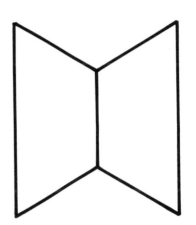

THESE ARE **NOT** YACKS.

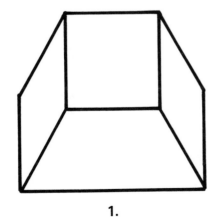

1.

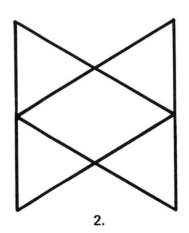

2.

CIRCLE THE YACKS.

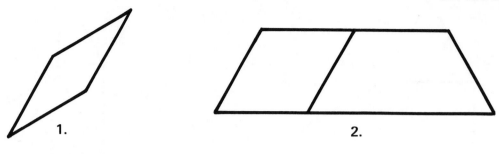

1.

2.

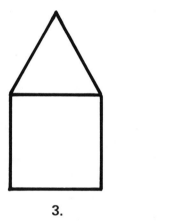

3.

4.

5.

TITLE: *1 Pattern Block*	TITLE: *2 Pattern Blocks*
WHAT GOES HERE?	WHAT GOES HERE?

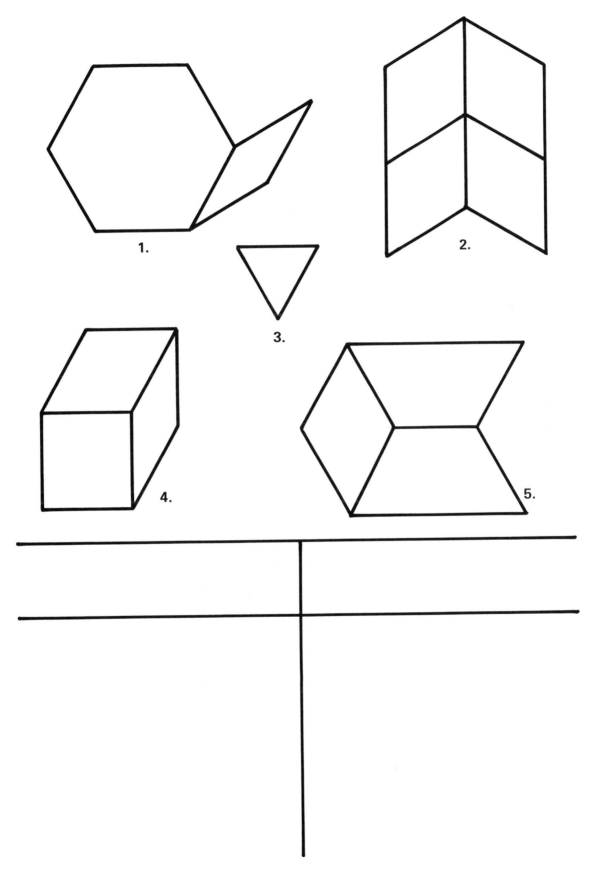

1.

2.

3.

4.

5.

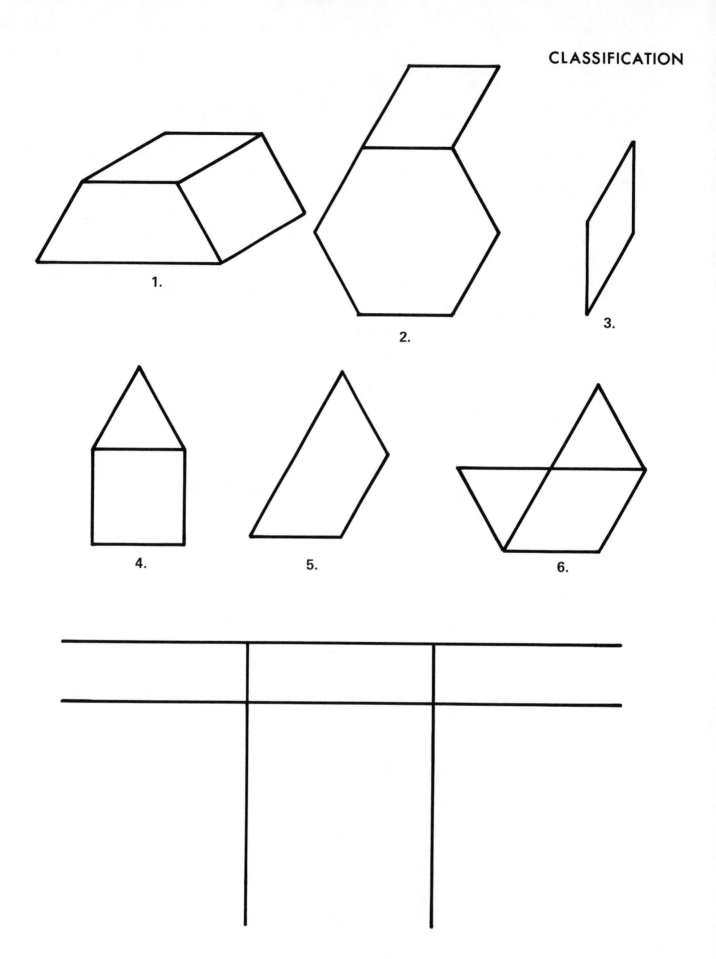

1.

2.

3.

4.

5.

6.

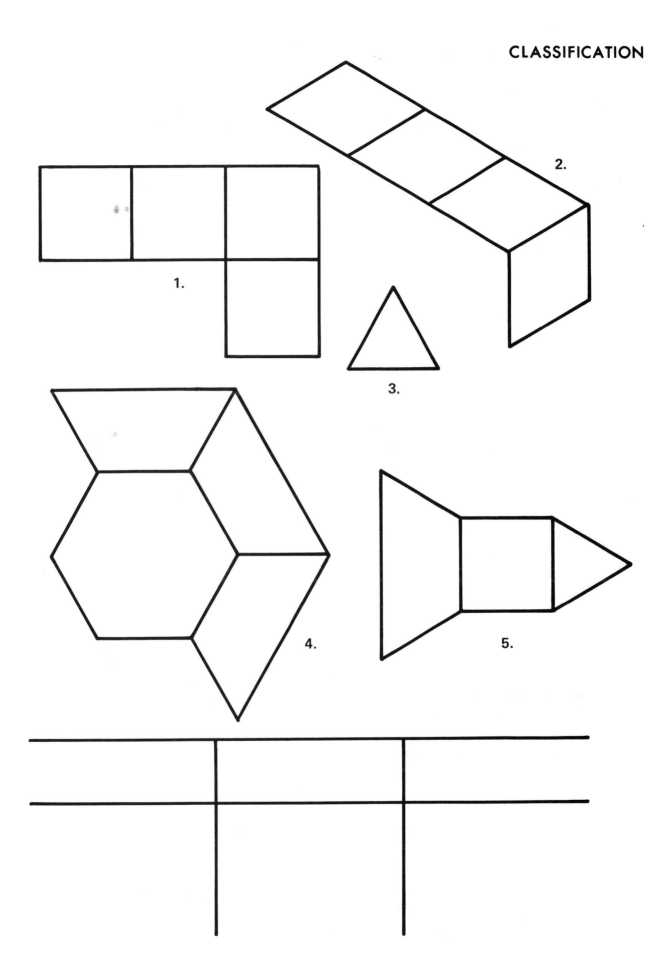

1.

2.

3.

4.

5.

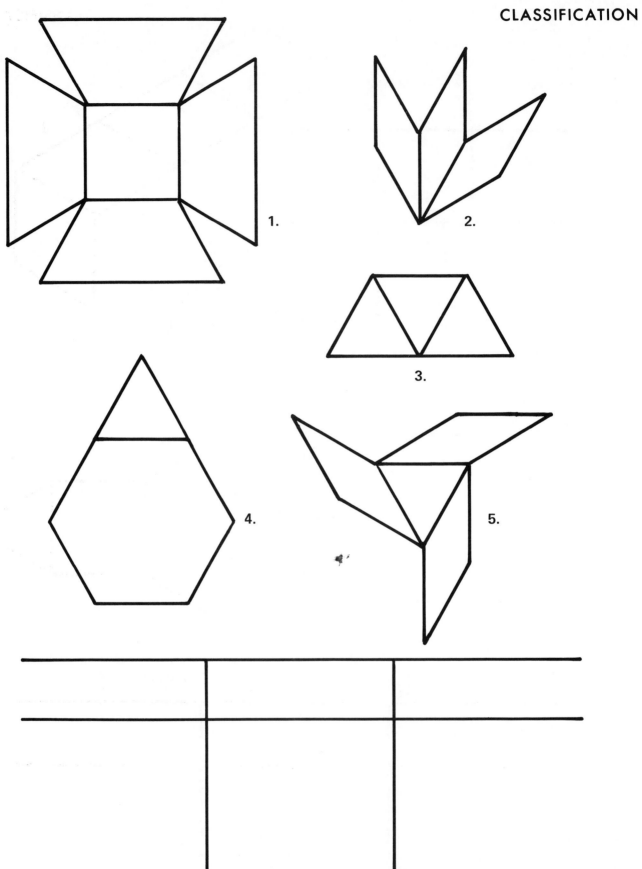

1.

2.

3.

4.

5.

MIRROR IMAGES

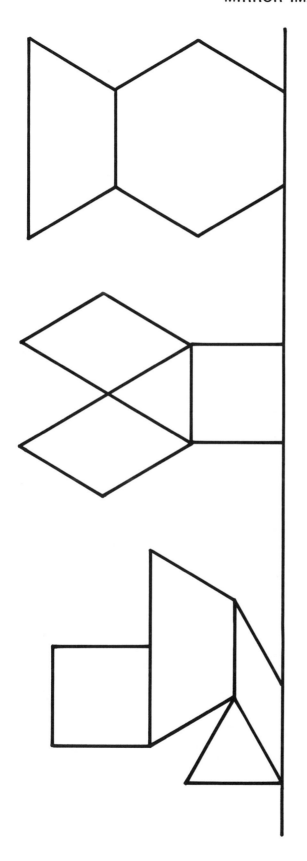

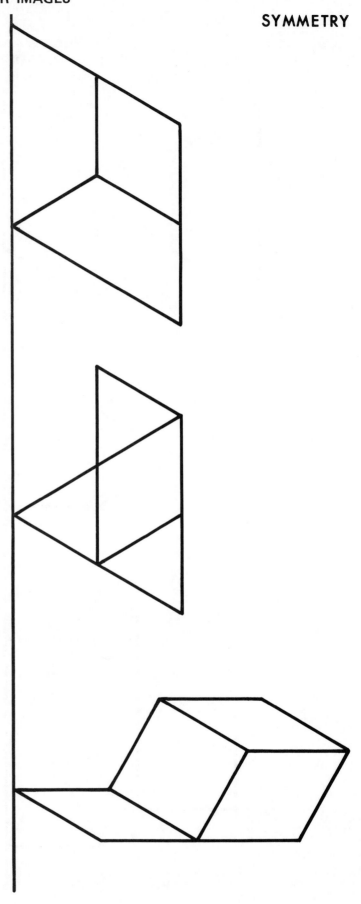

MIRROR TWINS

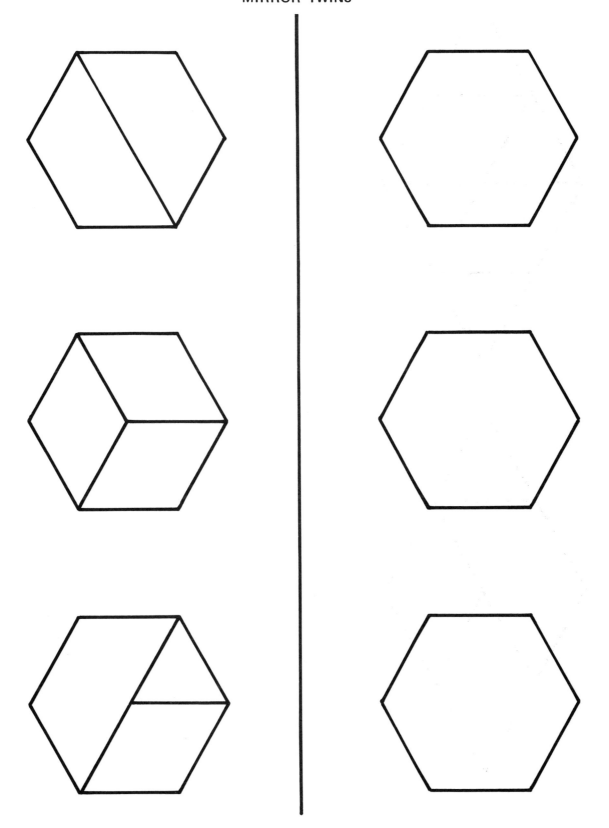

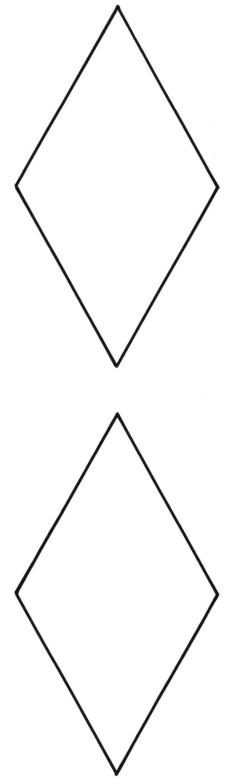

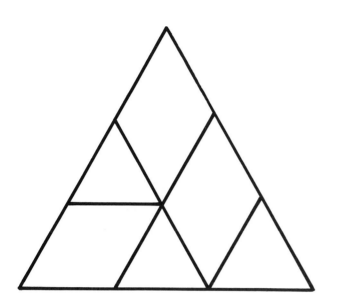

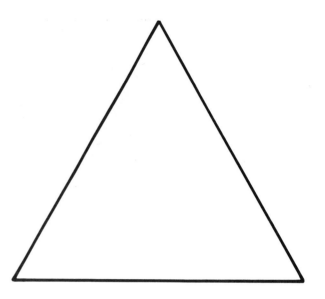

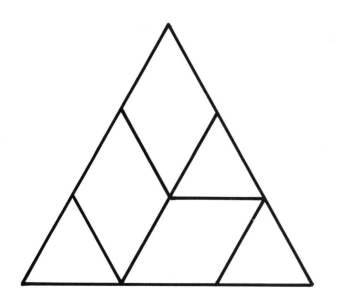

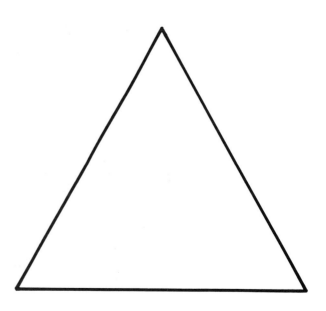

DO THESE SHAPES HAVE MIRROR SYMMETRY?

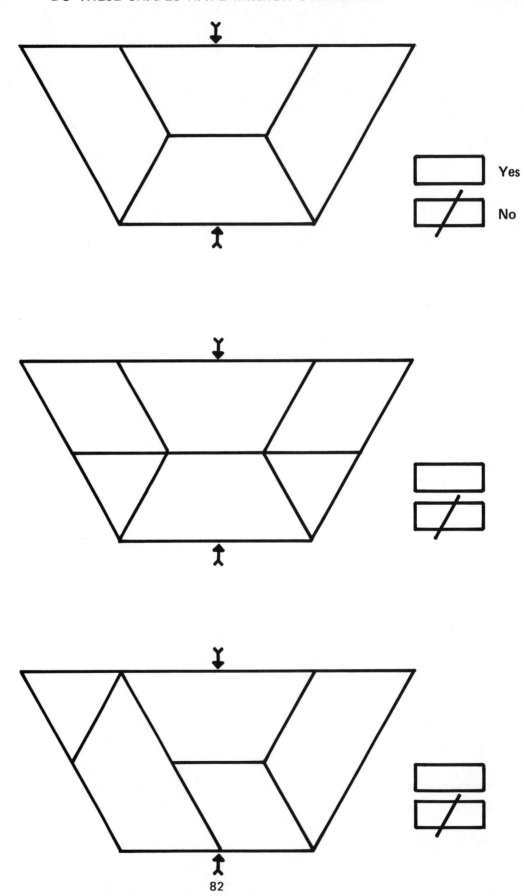

Yes

No

DO THESE SHAPES HAVE MIRROR SYMMETRY?

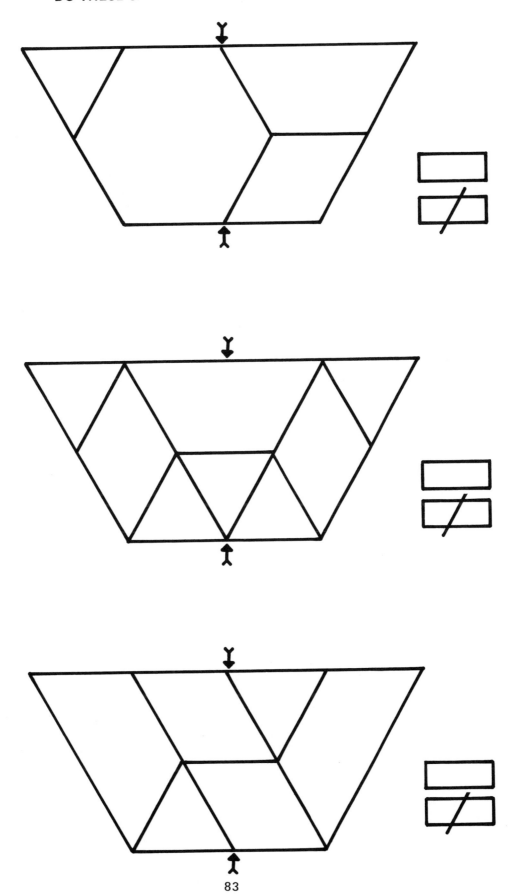

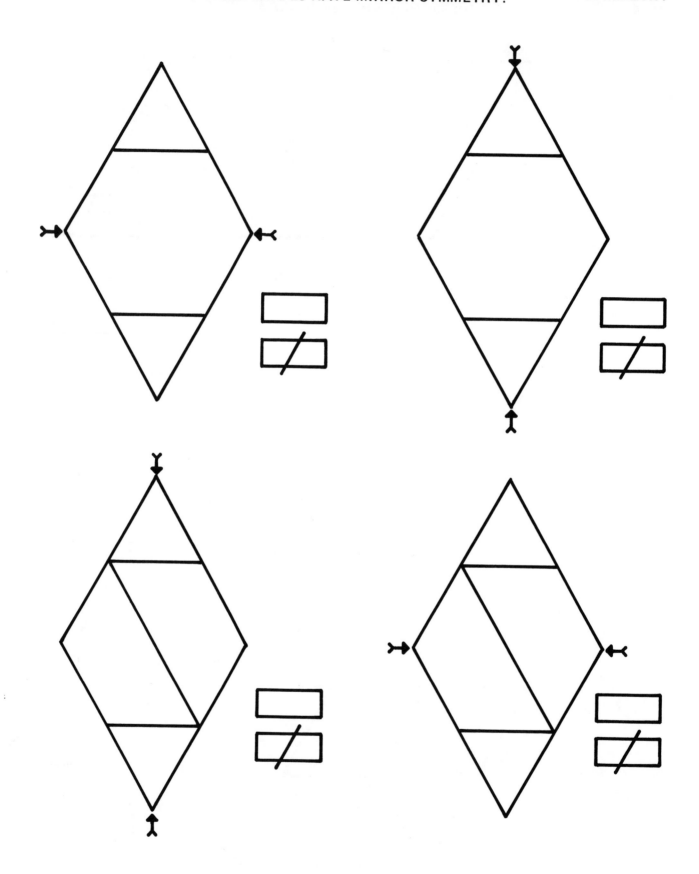

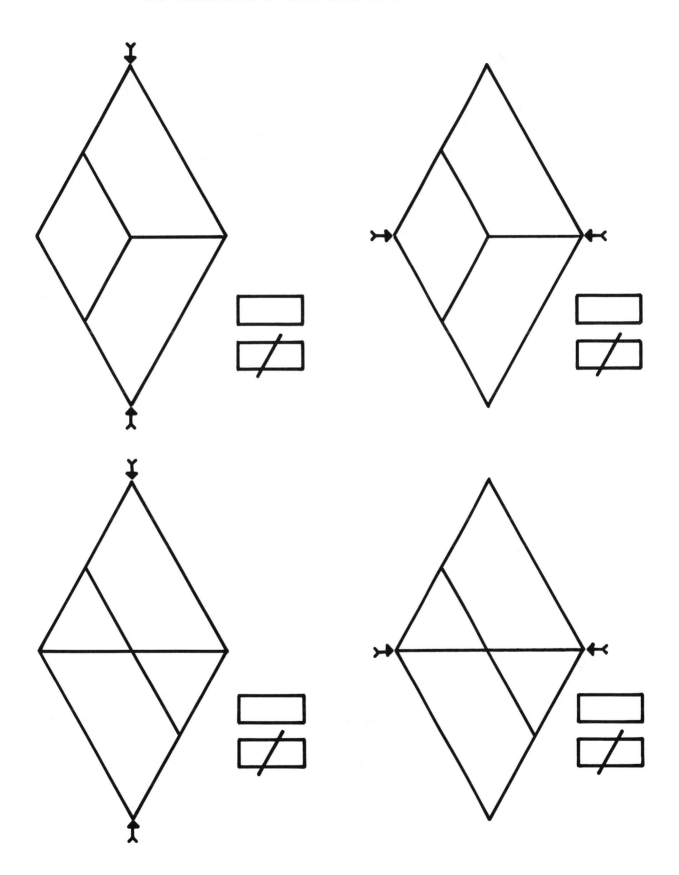

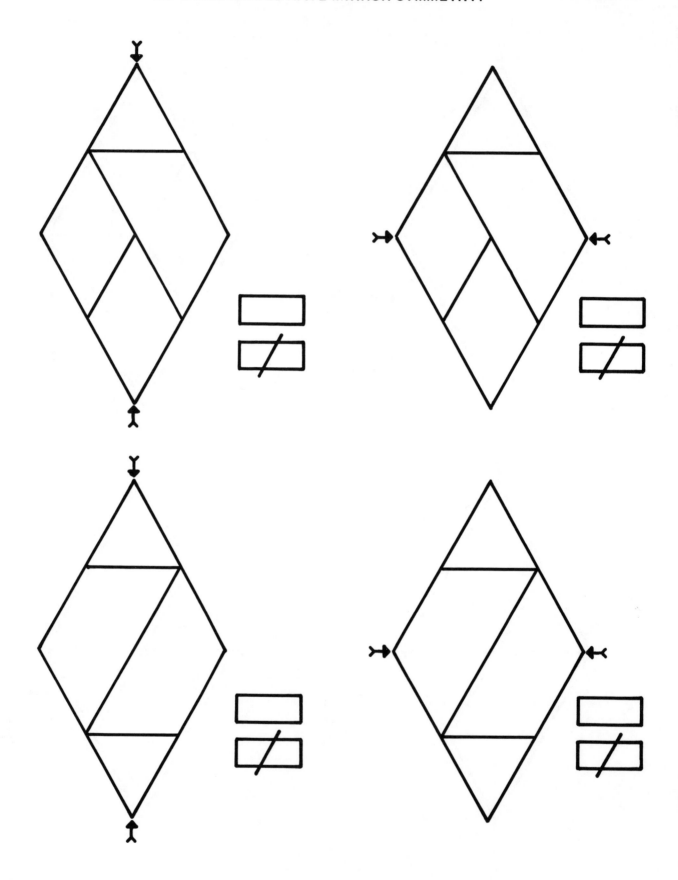

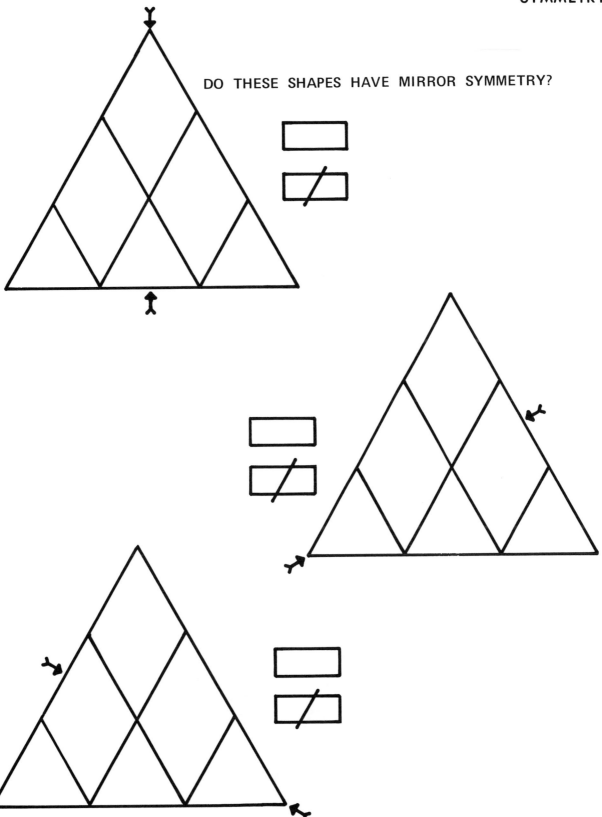

DO THESE SHAPES HAVE MIRROR SYMMETRY?

87

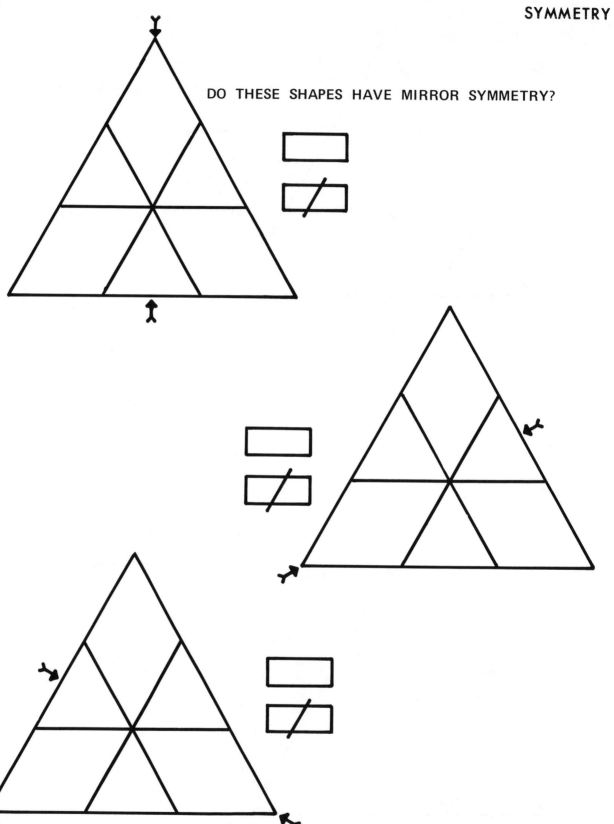

DO THESE SHAPES HAVE MIRROR SYMMETRY?

HOW MANY LINES OF SYMMETRY?

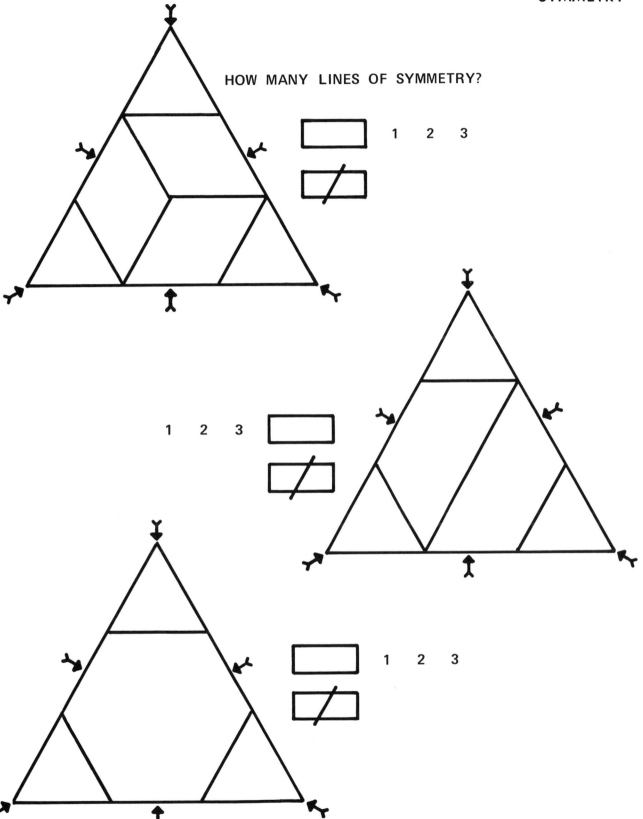

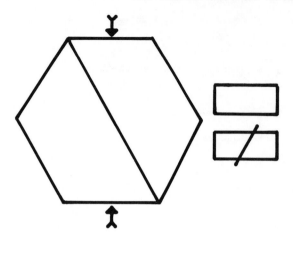

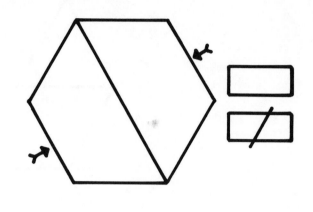

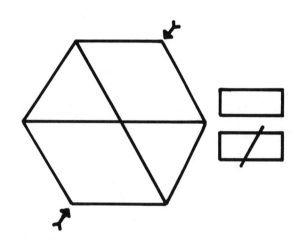

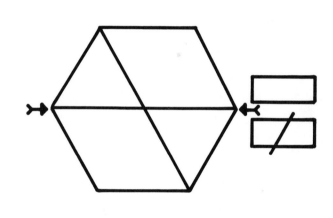

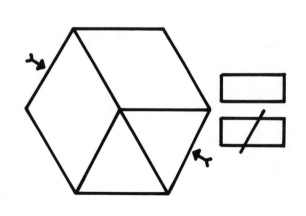

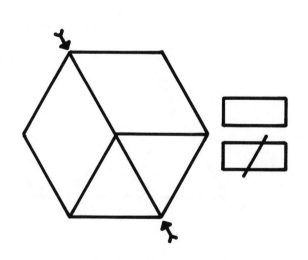

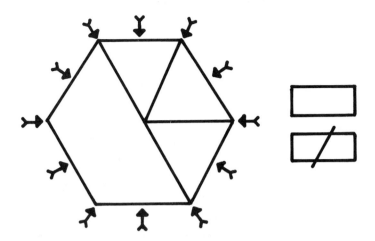

1　　2　　3　　4　　5　　6

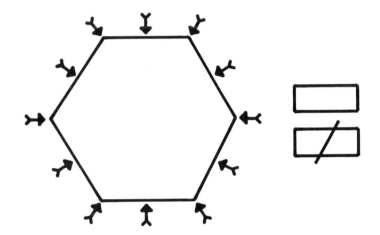

1　　2　　3　　4　　5　　6

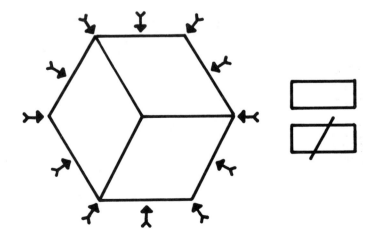

1　　2　　3　　4　　5　　6

DO THESE SHAPES HAVE ROTATIONAL SYMMETRY?

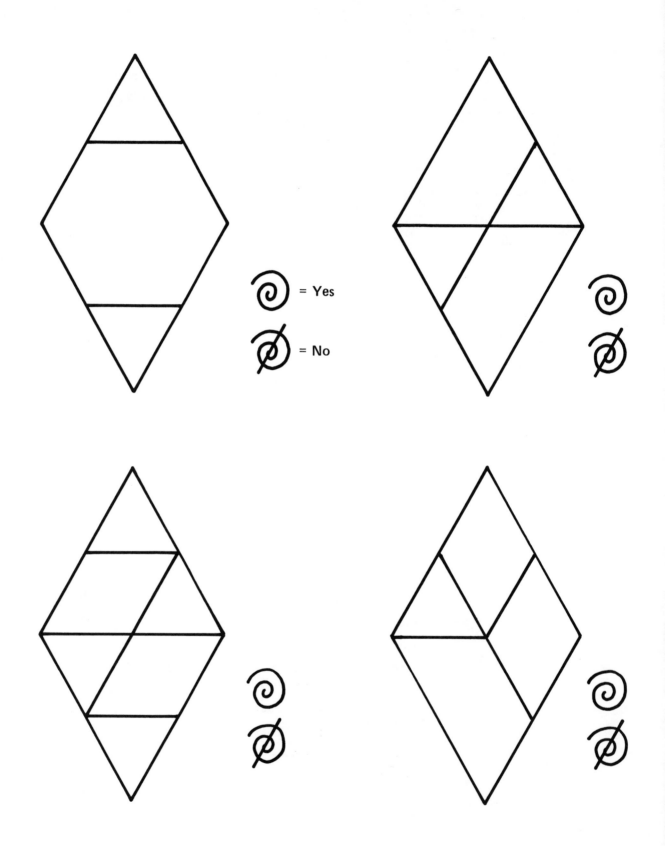

= Yes

= No

DO THESE SHAPES HAVE ROTATIONAL SYMMETRY?

 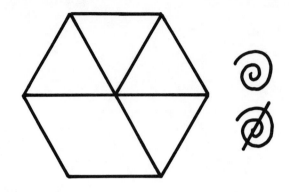

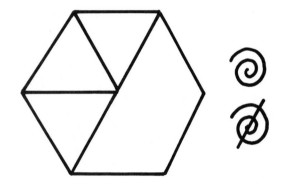 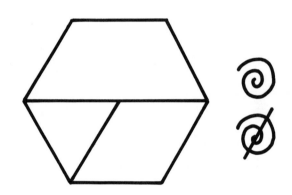

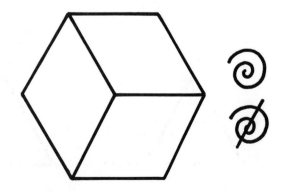 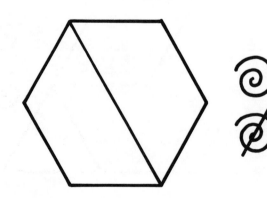

DO THESE SHAPES HAVE ROTATIONAL SYMMETRY?

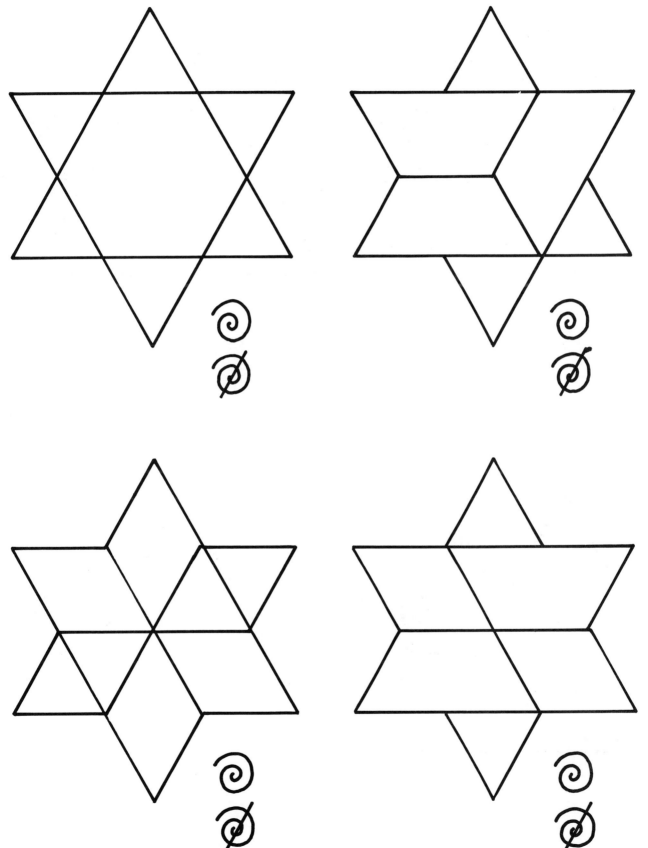

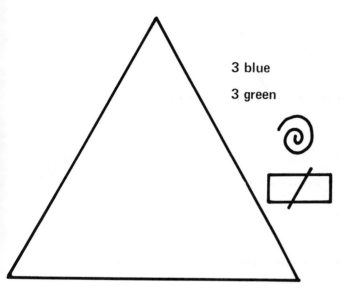

3 blue

3 green

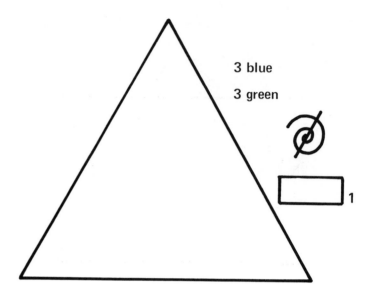

3 blue

3 green

1

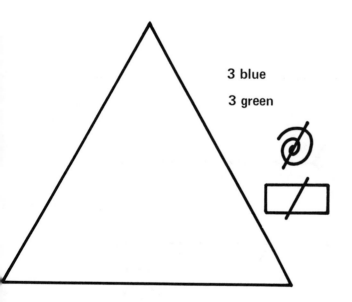

3 blue

3 green

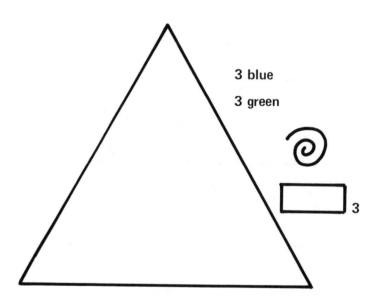

3 blue

3 green

3

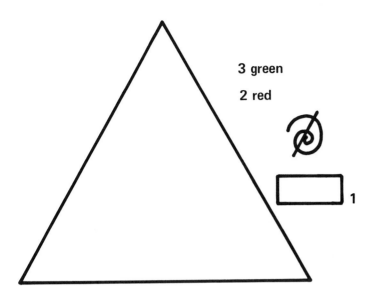

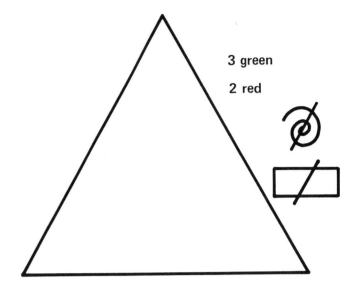

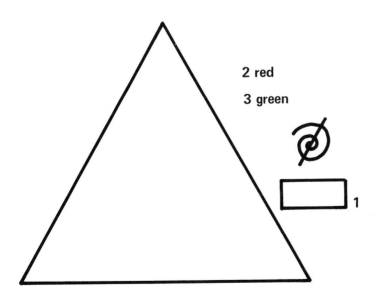

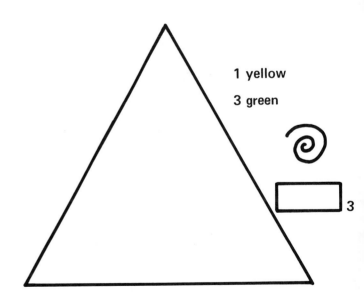

SNAIL STRATEGY

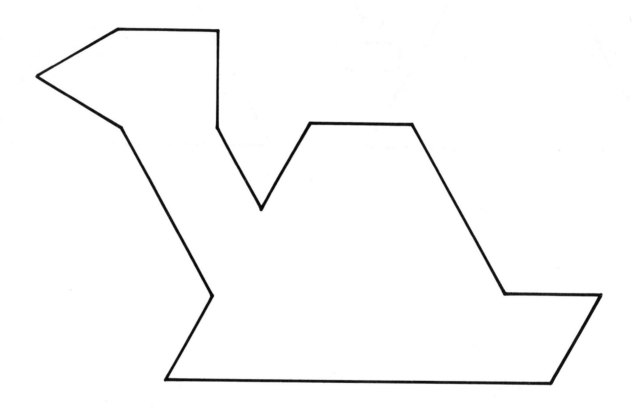

HOW MANY BLOCKS COVER THE SNAIL?

1	2	3	4	5	6	7	8	9	10
11	12	13	14	15	16	17	18	19	20
21	22	23	24	25	26	27	28	29	30

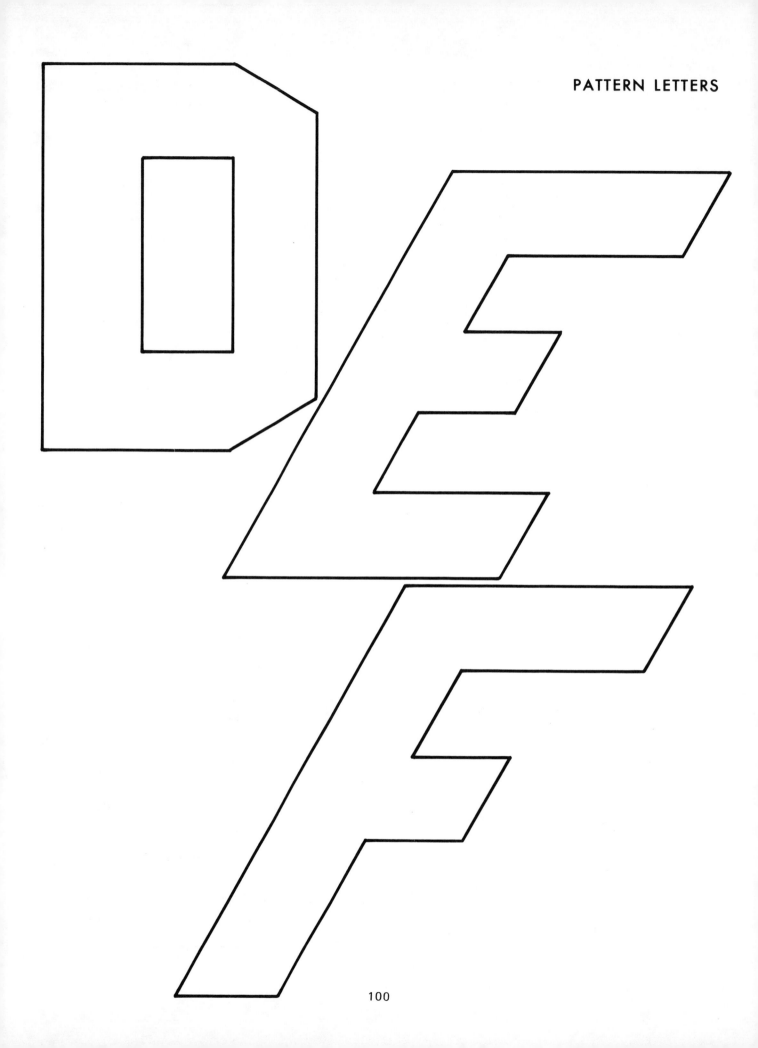

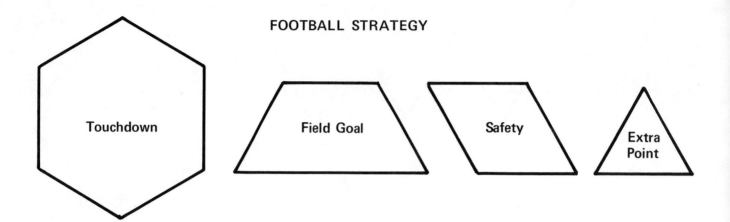

FOOTBALL STRATEGY

Touchdown   Field Goal   Safety   Extra Point

Name 6 ways to score 12 points.

1)   2)   3)

4)   5)   6)

Name 12 ways to score 18 points.

1)   2)   3)

4)   5)   6)

7)   8)   9)

10)   11)   12)

IF 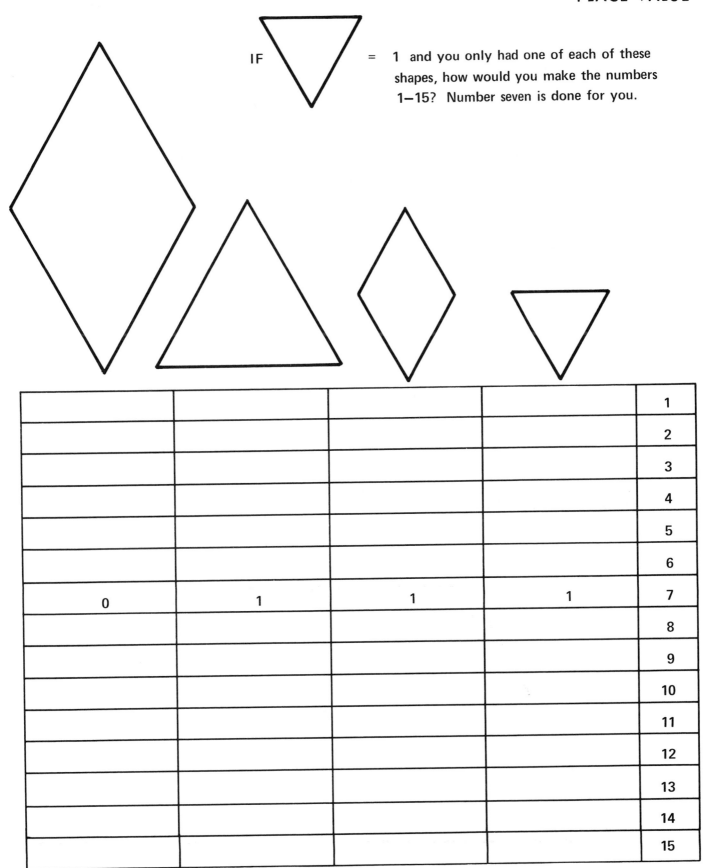 = 1 and you only had one of each of these shapes, how would you make the numbers 1–15? Number seven is done for you.

				1
				2
				3
				4
				5
				6
0	1	1	1	7
				8
				9
				10
				11
				12
				13
				14
				15

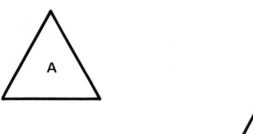

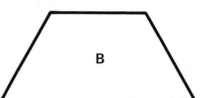

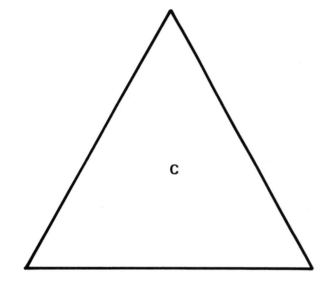

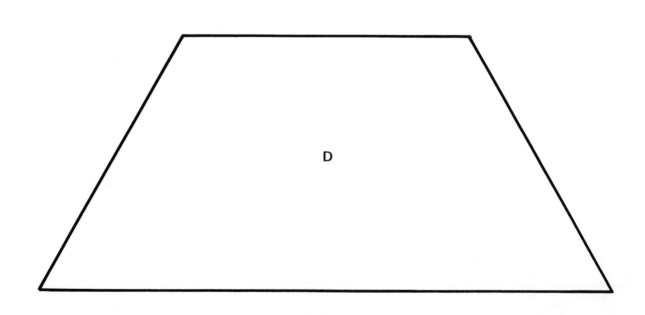

A =   1

B = ____

C = ____

D = ____

IF YOU ONLY HAD 2 A SHAPES, 2 B SHAPES, 2 C SHAPES,

AND 2 D SHAPES, HOW WOULD YOU MAKE THESE

NUMBERS? NUMBER 7 IS DONE FOR YOU.

Number of D's	Number of C's	Number of B's	Number of A's	
				1
				2
				3
				4
				5
				6
0	0	2	1	7
				8
				9
				10
				11
				12
				13
				14
				15
				27
				28
				50
				54
				80

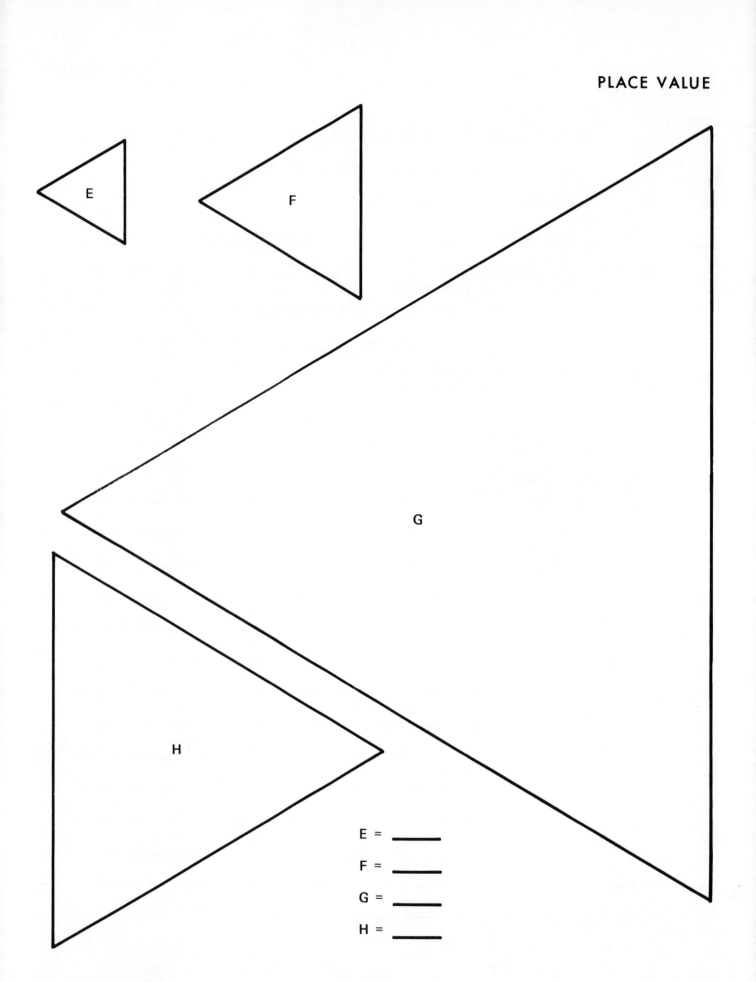

E = _____

F = _____

G = _____

H = _____

IF YOU ONLY HAD 3 E's, 3 F's, 3 G's, AND 3 H's, HOW WOULD YOU

MAKE THESE NUMBERS? NUMBER SEVEN IS DONE FOR YOU.

Number of H's	Number of G's	Number of F's	Number of E's	
				1
				2
				3
				4
				5
				6
0	0	1	3	7
				8
				9
				10
				11
				12
				13
				14
				15
				16
				17
				25
				64
				100

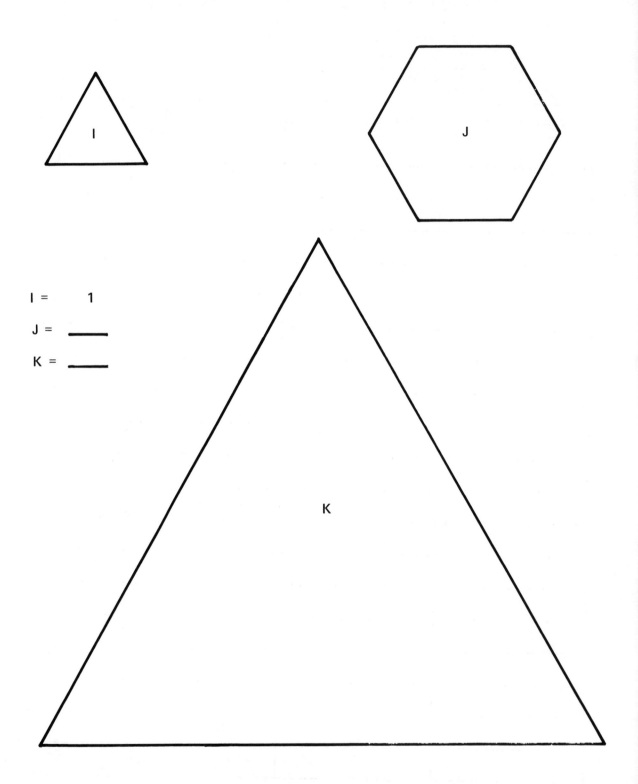

I =   1

J = _____

K = _____

PLACE VALUE

IF YOU ONLY HAD 5 I's, 5 J's AND 5 K's, HOW WOULD YOU

MAKE THESE NUMBERS? NUMBER 7 IS DONE FOR YOU.

K's	J's	I's		K's	J's	I's	
			1				21
			2				22
			3				23
			4				24
			5				25
			6				26
0	1	1	7				27
			8				28
			9				29
			10				30
			11				31
			12				32
			13				33
			14				34
			15				35
			16				36
			17				37
			18				38
			19				39
			20				40

113

LAST BLOCK RETURNS

The activity is played with the same rules as on Page 28. The only difference is that the players completely fill the hexagon first with blocks of their choice. Then these blocks are removed and are the only blocks that are allowed to be chosen by the players as they play.

AGAIN, WINNER IS THE PLAYER WHO PLACES THE LAST BLOCK THAT IS POSSIBLE TO BE PLAYED, SINCE IT IS POSSIBLE THAT NOT ALL THE BLOCKS WILL BE PLAYABLE.

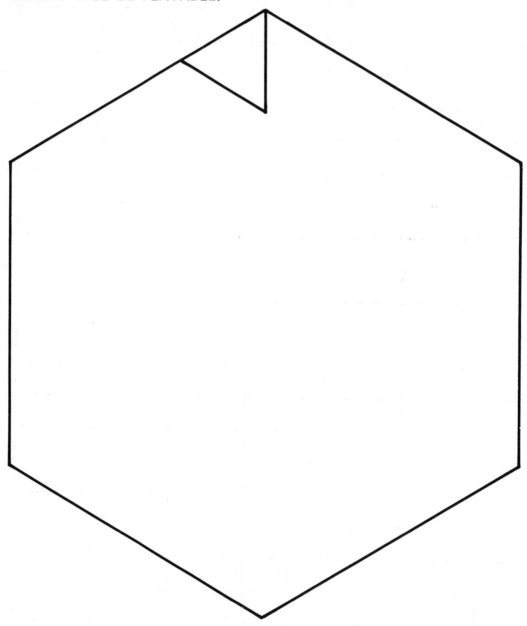

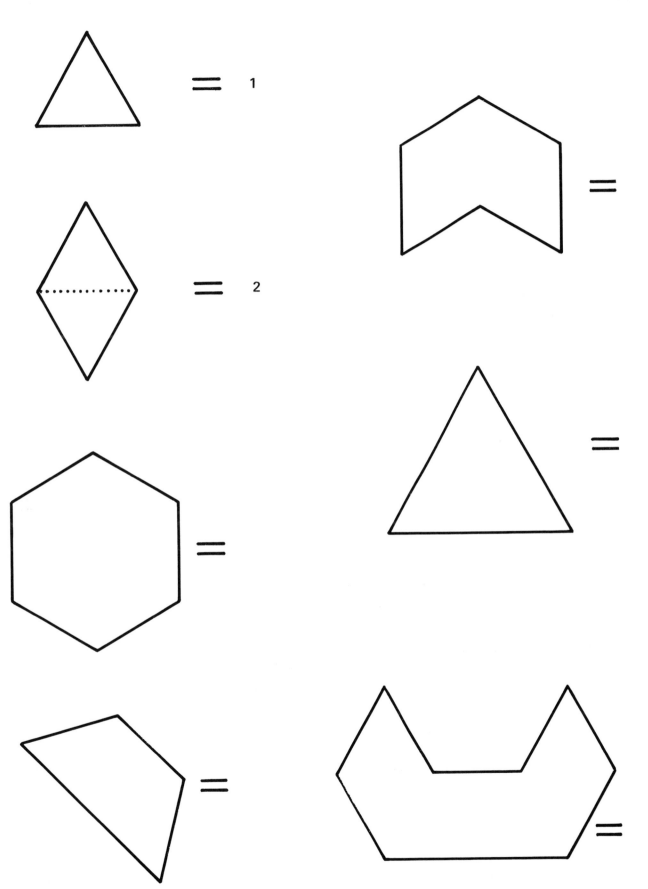

= 1

= 2

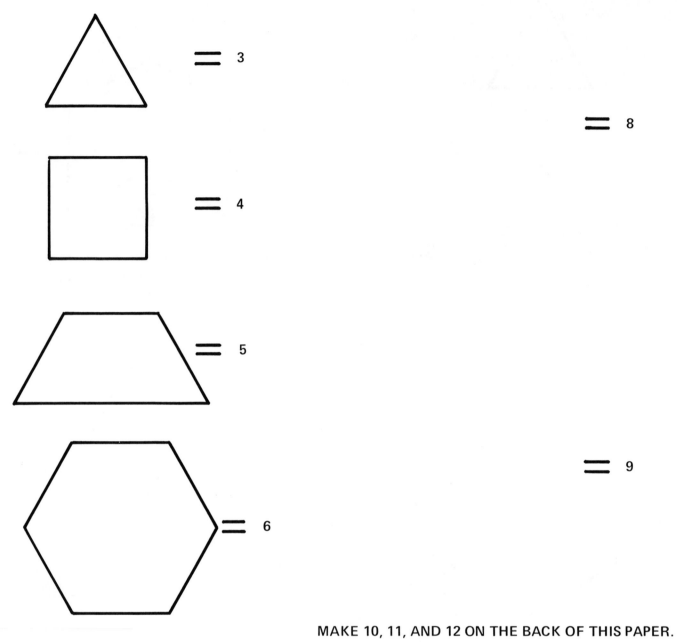

= 3

= 8

= 4

= 5

= 9

= 6

MAKE 10, 11, AND 12 ON THE BACK OF THIS PAPER.

= 7

1)

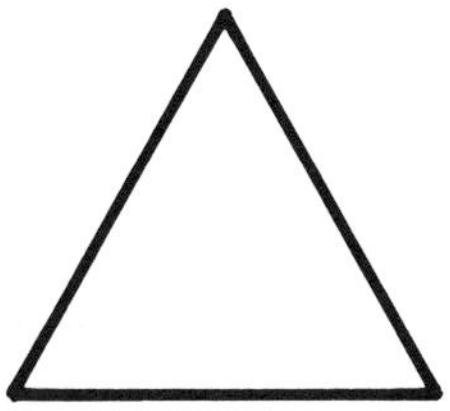

PERIMETER _____

AREA _____

2)

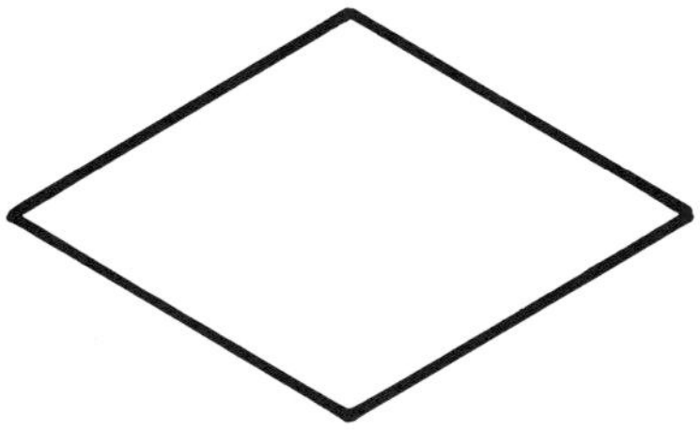

PERIMETER _____

AREA _____

3)

PERIMETER _____

AREA _____

4)

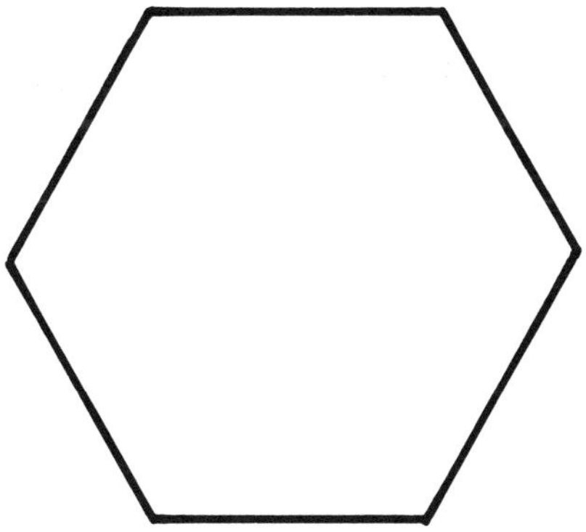

PERIMETER _____

AREA _____

5)

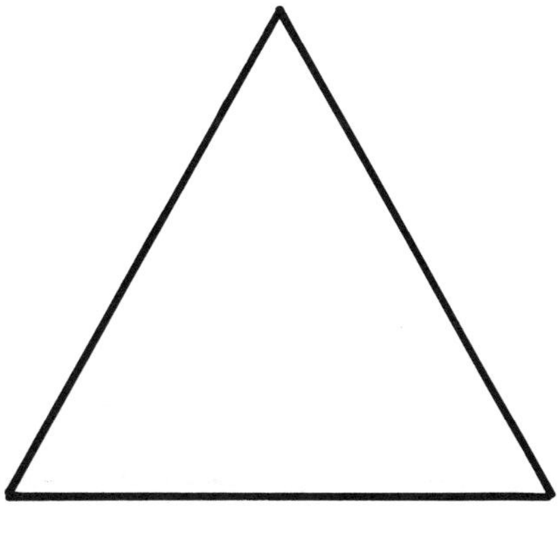

PERIMETER _____

AREA _____

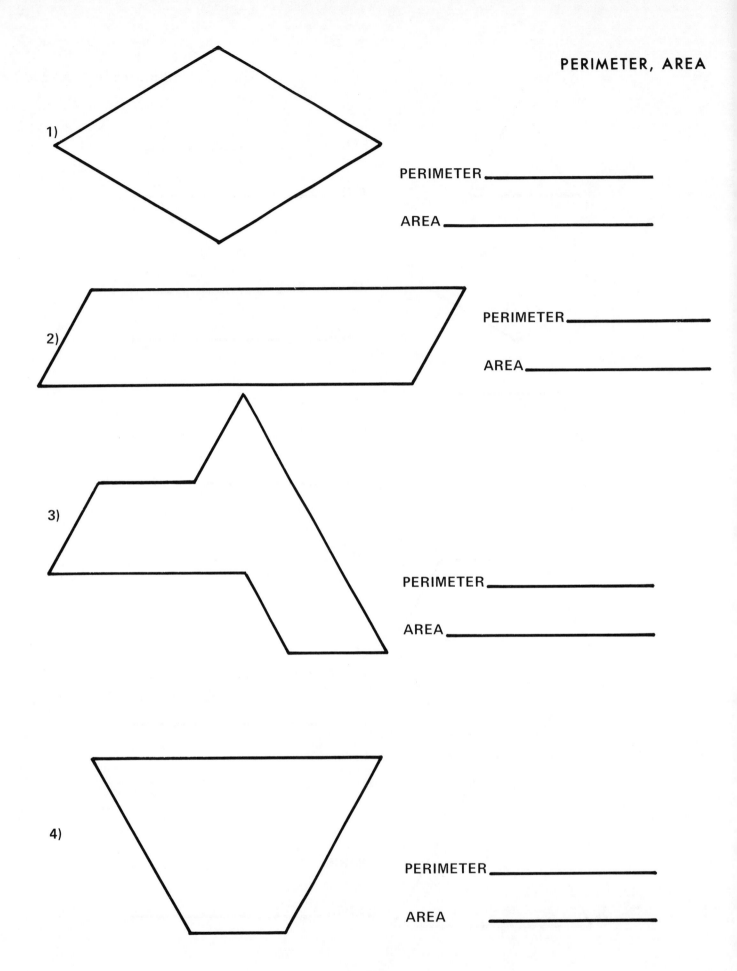

1)

PERIMETER _____

AREA _____

2)

PERIMETER _____

AREA _____

3)

PERIMETER _____

AREA _____

4)

PERIMETER _____

AREA _____

If GREEN = 1 unit of area, draw the following polygons:

1. Area = 4   Perimeter = 6
2. A = 6   P = 6
3. A = 6   P = 8
4. A = 9   P = 9
5. A = 8   P = 8

Completed work should
look like this:

Area = 12
Perimeter = 10

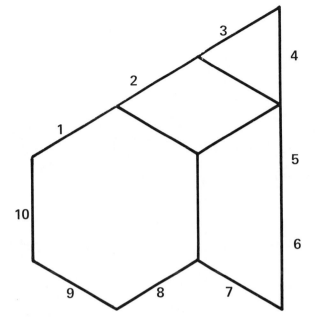

If BLUE = 1 unit of area, draw the following polygons:

6. A = 3   P = 6
7. A = 3   P = 8
8. A = 4   P = 8
9. A = 8   P = 10
10. A = 4   P = 10

If RED = 1 unit of area, draw the following polygons:

11. A = 2   P = 8
12. A = 2   P = 6
13. A = 4   P = 10
14. A = 5   P = 17
15. A = 5   P = 13

If YELLOW = 1 unit of area, draw the following polygons:

16. A = 3   P = 12
17. A = 4   P = 14
18. A = 4½   P = 17
19. A = 4½   P = 15
20. A = 3   P = 20

HOW MANY PIECES?

	1	2	3	4
Square				
Triangle				
Blue Rhombus				
White Rhombus				
Hexagon				
Trapezoid				

120

HOW MANY ORANGE SQUARES FILL EACH SQUARE?

3

2

1

4

HOW MANY GREEN TRIANGLES FILL EACH TRIANGLE?

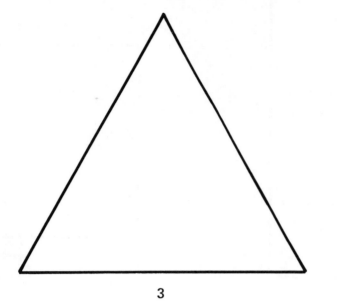

3

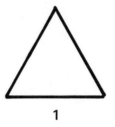

1

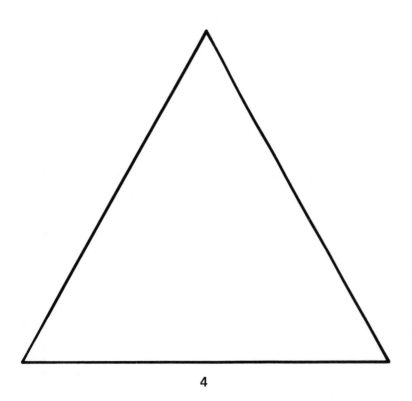

4

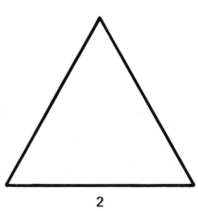

2

1 is the first

triangular number

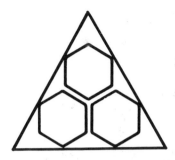

3 is the second

triangular number

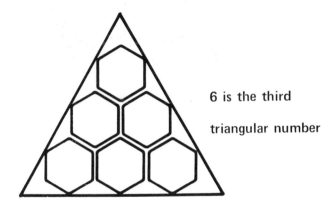

6 is the third

triangular number

1) USING HEXAGONS SEE IF YOU CAN
   MAKE THE FOURTH TRIANGULAR NUMBER.

   HOW MANY HEXAGONS DID YOU USE?_____

2) WHAT IS THE FIFTH
   TRIANGULAR NUMBER?

   _____

3) CAN YOU PREDICT THE EIGHTH
   TRIANGULAR NUMBER?

   WHAT IS IT? _____

4) WHAT IS THE TENTH
   TRIANGULAR NUMBER?

   _____

1   THE FIRST HEXAGONAL NUMBER

THE SECOND
HEXAGONAL
NUMBER

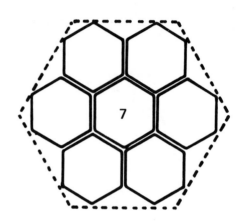

1) CAN YOU MAKE THE THIRD
HEXAGONAL NUMBER?

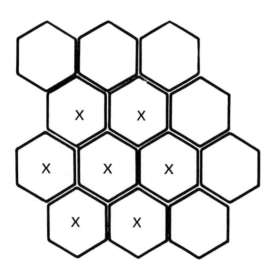

2) THE FOURTH HEXAGONAL
NUMBER IS?

_____

HOW MANY HEXAGONS DID YOU USE?_____

2 BLOCKS 1 COLOR

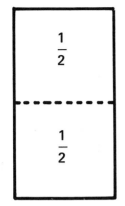

2 BLOCKS 1 COLOR

2 BLOCKS 1 COLOR

2 BLOCKS 1 COLOR

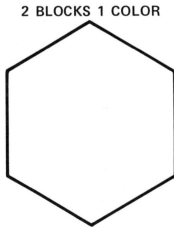

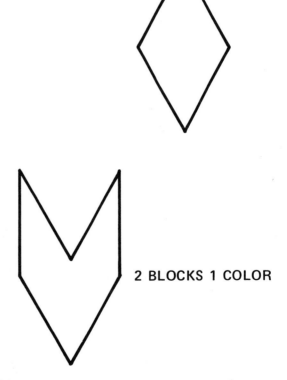

2 BLOCKS 1 COLOR

2 BLOCKS 1 COLOR

$$\frac{1}{3}$$

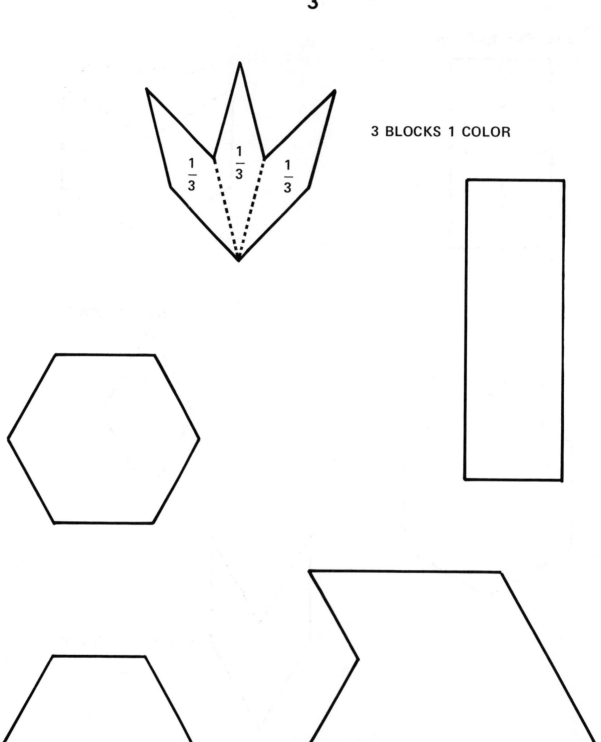

3 BLOCKS 1 COLOR

$$\frac{1}{4}$$

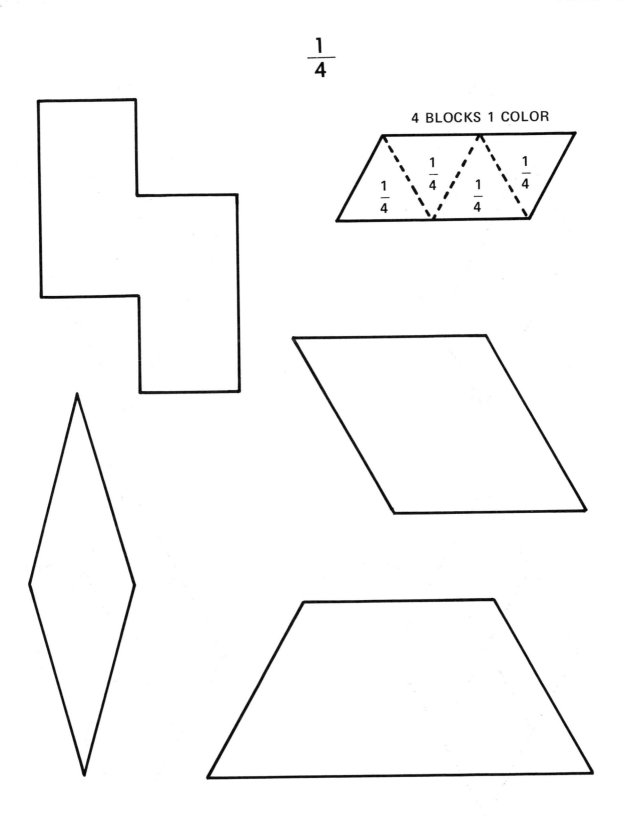

4 BLOCKS 1 COLOR

$\frac{1}{4}$ $\frac{1}{4}$ $\frac{1}{4}$ $\frac{1}{4}$

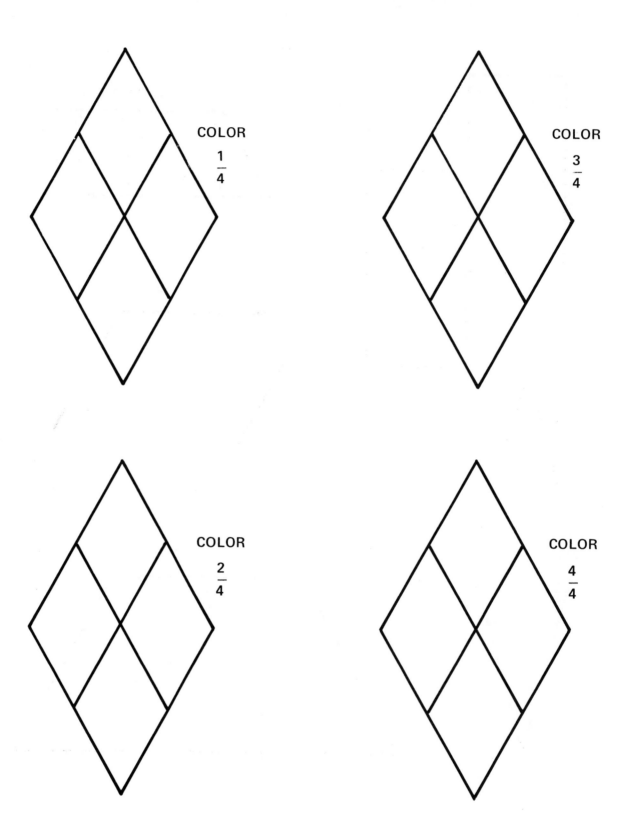

COLOR

$\dfrac{1}{4}$

COLOR

$\dfrac{3}{4}$

COLOR

$\dfrac{2}{4}$

COLOR

$\dfrac{4}{4}$

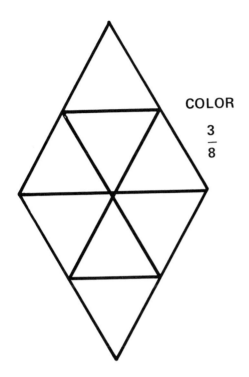

COLOR

$\dfrac{3}{8}$

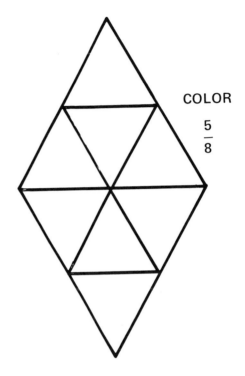

COLOR

$\dfrac{5}{8}$

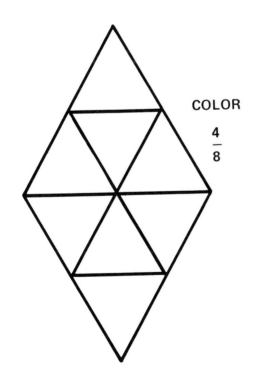

COLOR

$\dfrac{4}{8}$

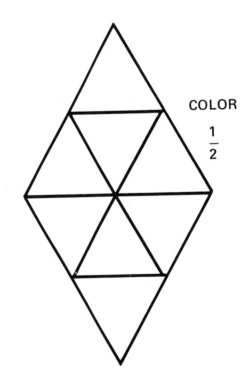

COLOR

$\dfrac{1}{2}$

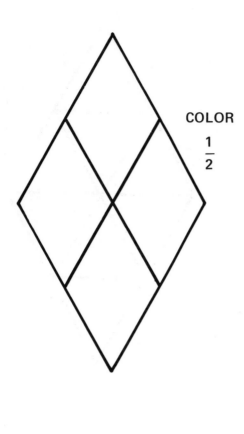

COLOR

$\frac{1}{2}$

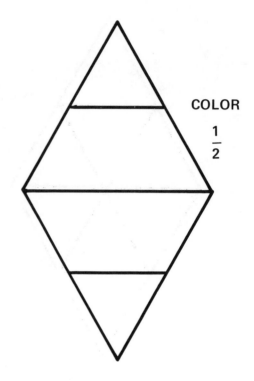

COLOR

$\frac{1}{2}$

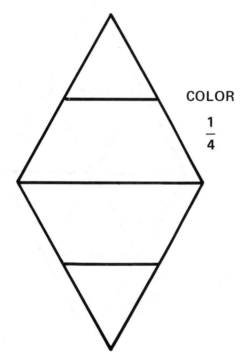

COLOR

$\frac{1}{4}$

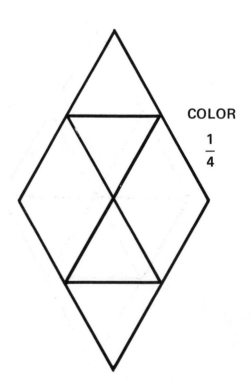

COLOR

$\frac{1}{4}$

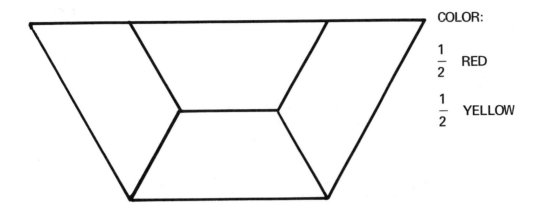

COLOR:

$\frac{1}{2}$ RED

$\frac{1}{2}$ YELLOW

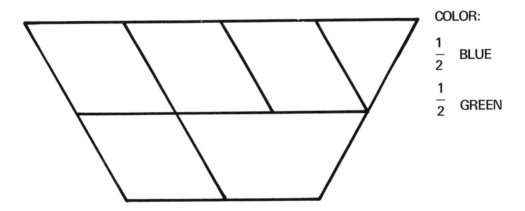

COLOR:

$\frac{1}{2}$ BLUE

$\frac{1}{2}$ GREEN

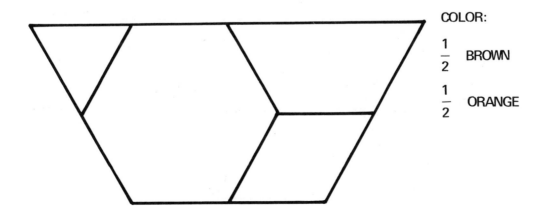

COLOR:

$\frac{1}{2}$ BROWN

$\frac{1}{2}$ ORANGE

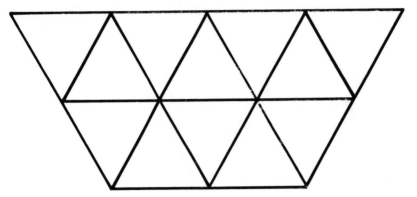

COLOR:

$\frac{1}{12}$ GREEN

$\frac{1}{2}$ RED

$\frac{1}{4}$ YELLOW

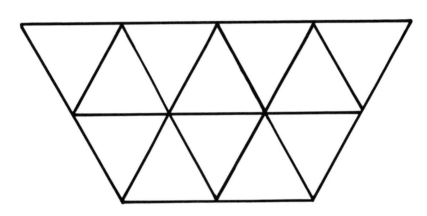

COLOR:

$\frac{7}{12}$ BLUE

$\frac{5}{12}$ ORANGE

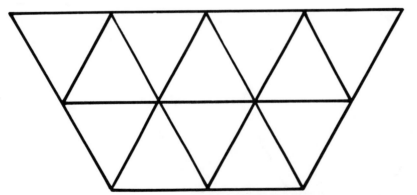

COLOR:

$\frac{6}{12}$ RED

$\frac{1}{2}$ ORANGE

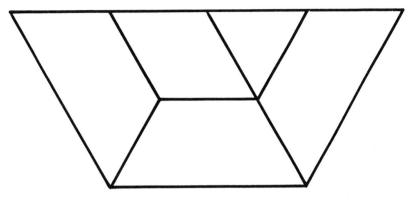

COLOR:

$\frac{1}{2}$ PURPLE

$\frac{1}{4}$ RED

$\frac{1}{6}$ ORANGE

$\frac{1}{12}$ PINK

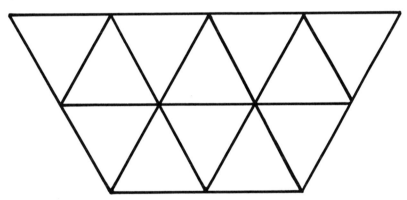

COLOR:

$\frac{1}{2}$ BLUE

$\frac{1}{3}$ PINK

$\frac{1}{6}$ YELLOW

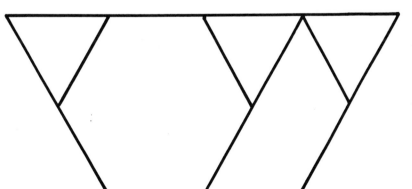

COLOR:

$\frac{3}{12}$ ORANGE

$\frac{3}{4}$ BROWN

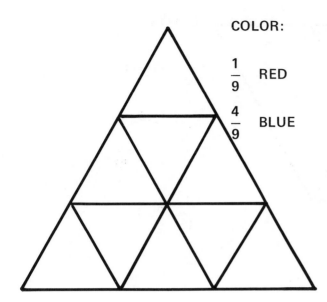

COLOR:

$\frac{1}{9}$ RED

$\frac{4}{9}$ BLUE

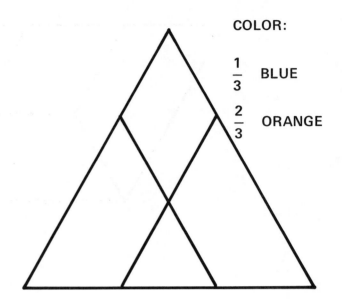

COLOR:

$\frac{1}{3}$ BLUE

$\frac{2}{3}$ ORANGE

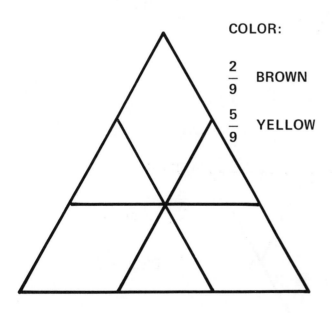

COLOR:

$\frac{2}{9}$ BROWN

$\frac{5}{9}$ YELLOW

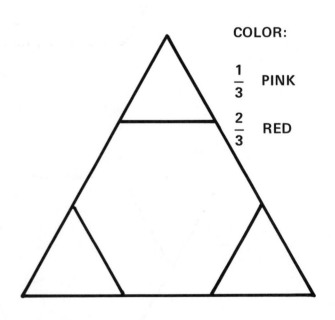

COLOR:

$\frac{1}{3}$ PINK

$\frac{2}{3}$ RED

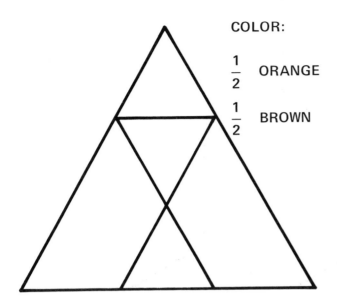

COLOR:

$\frac{1}{2}$ ORANGE

$\frac{1}{2}$ BROWN

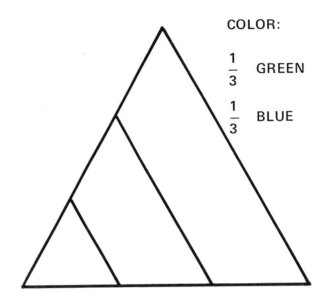

COLOR:

$\frac{1}{3}$ GREEN

$\frac{1}{3}$ BLUE

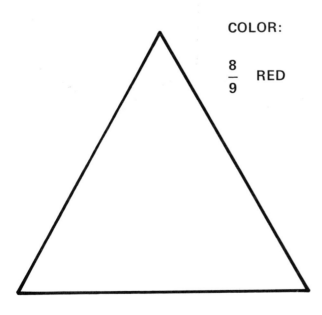

COLOR:

$\frac{8}{9}$ RED

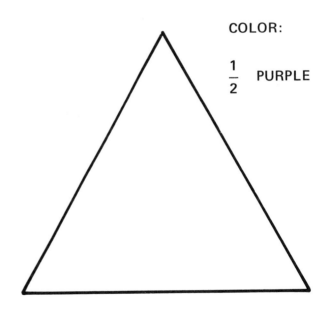

COLOR:

$\frac{1}{2}$ PURPLE

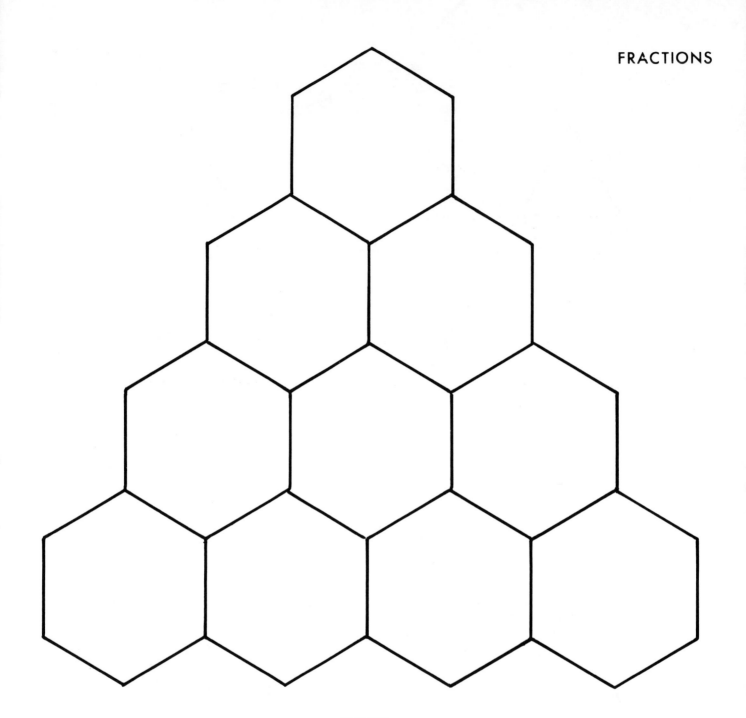

COLOR:

$\frac{1}{2}$ GREEN

$\frac{1}{10}$ ORANGE

$\frac{3}{10}$ BLUE

COLOR: .3 RED, .4 GREEN

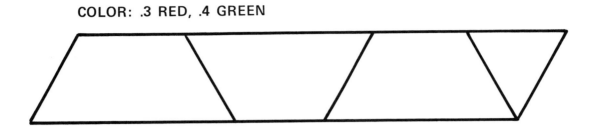

COLOR: .5 RED, .3 GREEN

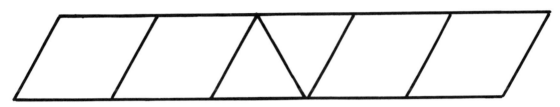

COLOR: .5 GREEN, .2 RED

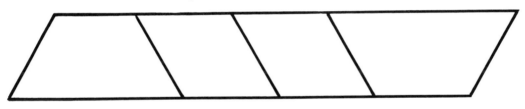

COLOR: .2 RED, .2 GREEN, .2 ORANGE, .2 BLUE

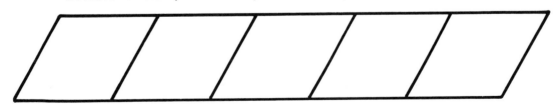

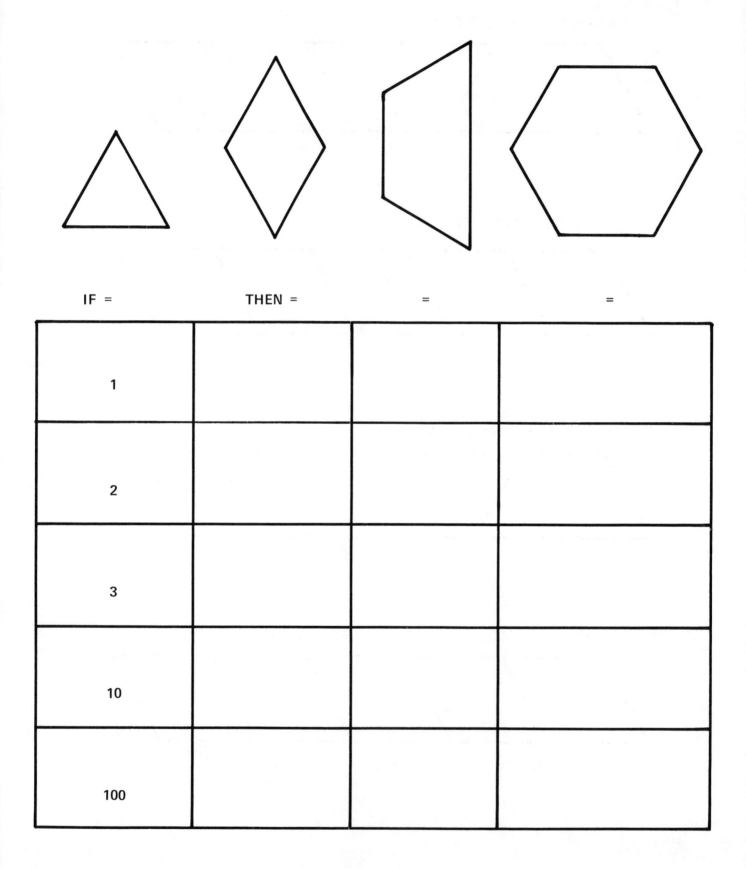

IF =   THEN =   =   =

1			
2			
3			
10			
100			

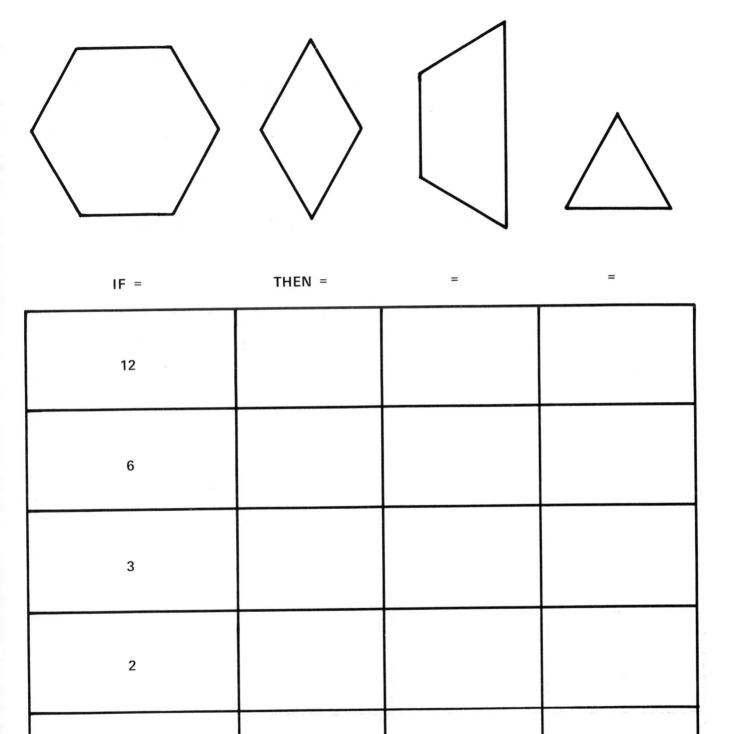

IF =   THEN =   =   =

12			
6			
3			
2			
1			

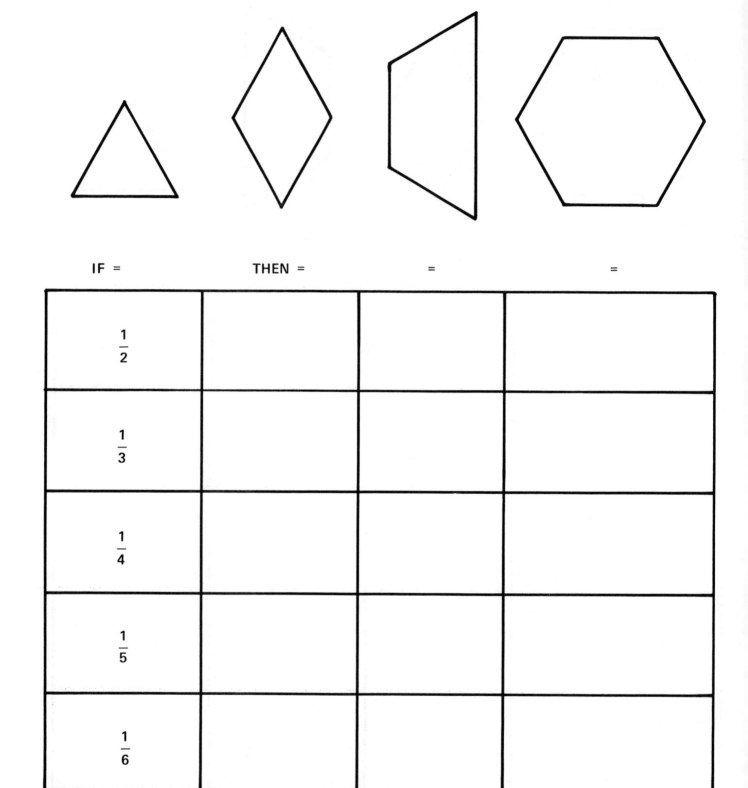

IF =   THEN =   =   =

$\dfrac{1}{2}$			
$\dfrac{1}{3}$			
$\dfrac{1}{4}$			
$\dfrac{1}{5}$			
$\dfrac{1}{6}$			

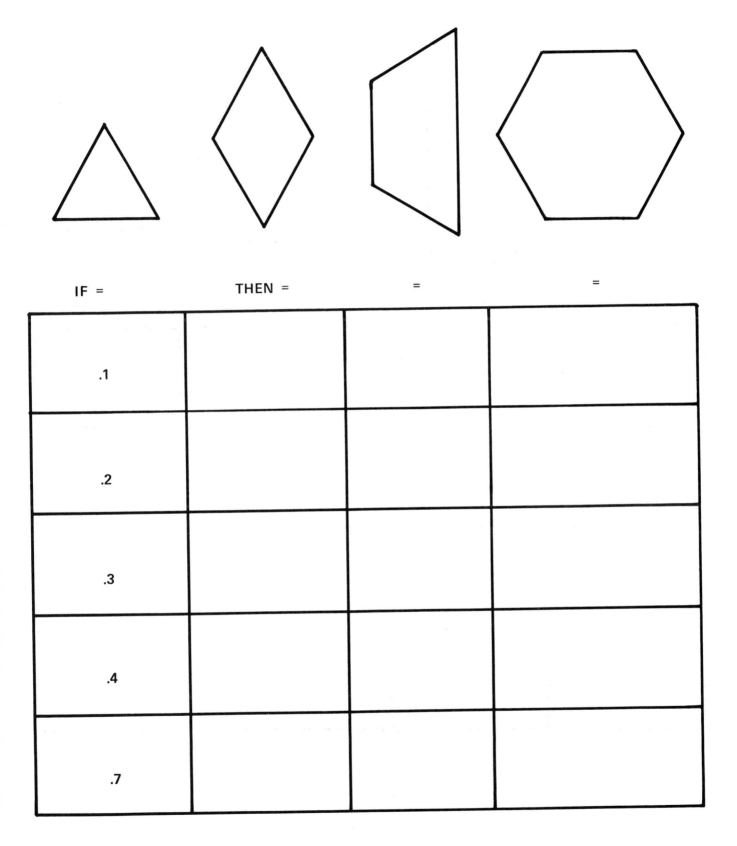

IF =   THEN =   =   =

.1			
.2			
.3			
.4			
.7			

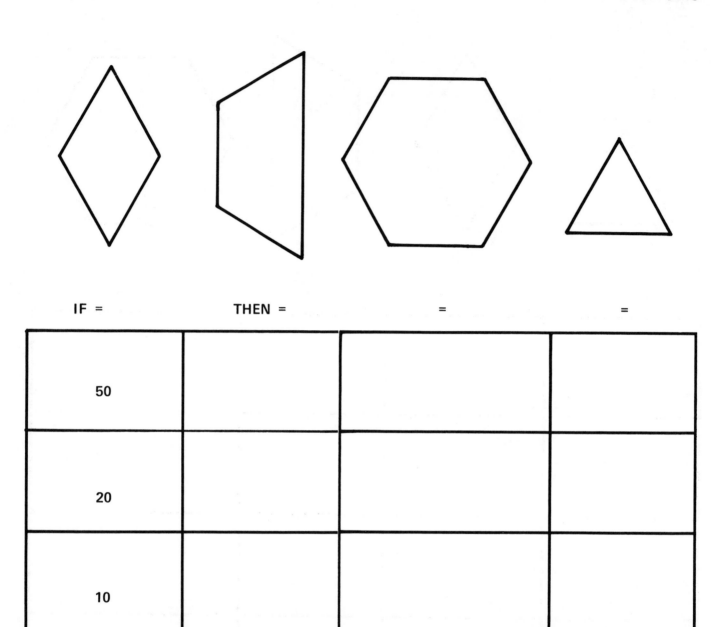

IF =   THEN =   =   =

50			
20			
10			
2			
1			

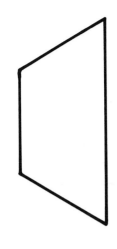 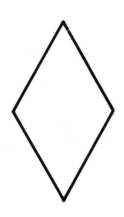  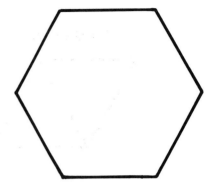

IF =	THEN =	=	=
30			
$\frac{3}{5}$			
$\frac{3}{10}$			
$\frac{1}{2}$			
$\frac{1}{4}$			

RECIPROCALS

FIGURE "A"

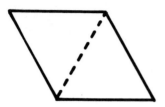

FIGURE "B"

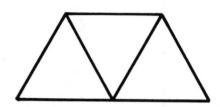

IF FIGURE "A" = $\frac{2}{2}$

THEN FIGURE "B" = $\frac{}{2}$

IF FIGURE "B" = $\frac{3}{3}$

THEN FIGURE "A" = ———

FIGURE "D"

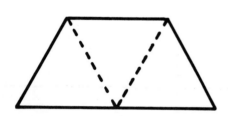

FIGURE "E"

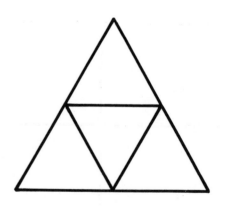

IF FIGURE "D" = $\frac{3}{3}$

THEN FIGURE "E" =

IF FIGURE "E" = $\frac{4}{4}$

THEN FIGURE "D" =

A

B

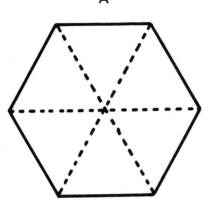

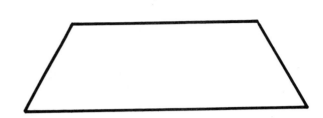

IF "A" = $\dfrac{6}{6}$ THEN "B" =

IF "B" = $\dfrac{5}{5}$ THEN "A" =

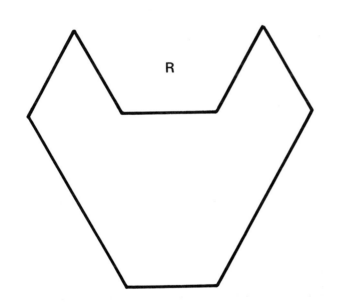

R

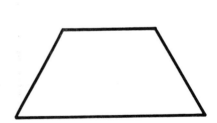

S

IF "R" = 1   THEN "S" =

IF "S" = 1   THEN "R" =

A

B

C

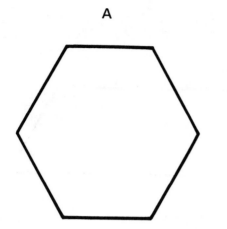
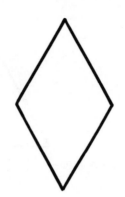
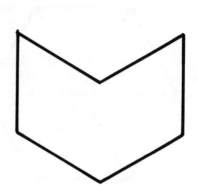

	AREA	THEN A=	THEN B=	THEN C=
IF	A = 1	1		
IF	B = 1		1	
IF	C = 1			1

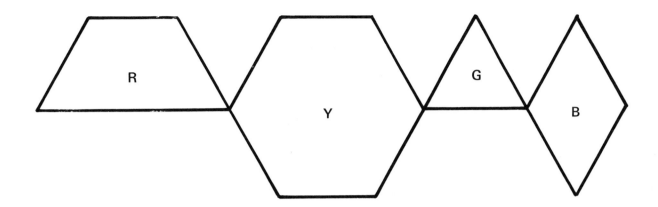

		THEN "G" =	THEN "B" =	THEN "R" =	THEN "Y" =
1)	IF "G" = 12	12			
2)	IF "B" = 12		12		
3)	IF "R" = 12			12	
4)	IF "Y" = 12				12

		THEN "G" =	THEN "B" =	THEN "R" =	THEN "Y" =
5)	IF "G" = 72	72			
6)	IF "B" = 72		72		
7)	IF "R" = 72			72	
8)	IF "Y" = 72				72

147

PATTERN BLOCKS

USE THE BLOCKS TO
HELP YOU IN SOLVING
THE PROBLEMS.

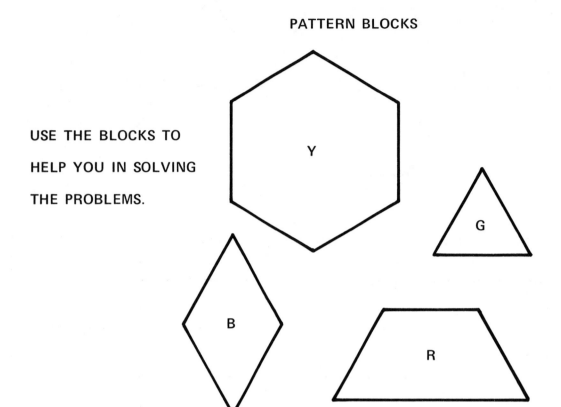

		THEN "G" =	THEN "B" =	THEN "R" =	THEN "Y" =
1)	IF "G" = 1	1			
2)	IF "B" = 1		1		
3)	IF "R" = 1			1	
4)	IF "Y" = 1				1

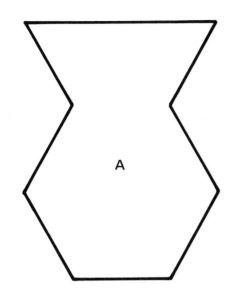

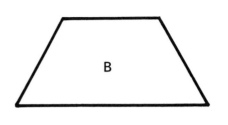

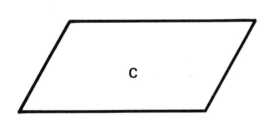

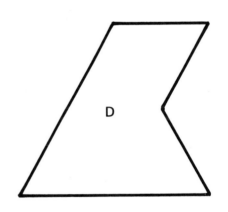

1) IF "A" = 1   THEN   "B" =   "C" =   "D" =

2) IF "B" = 1   THEN   "A" =   "C" =   "D" =

3) IF "C" = 1   THEN   "A" =   "B" =   "D" =

4) IF "D" = 1   THEN   "A" =   "B" =   "C" =

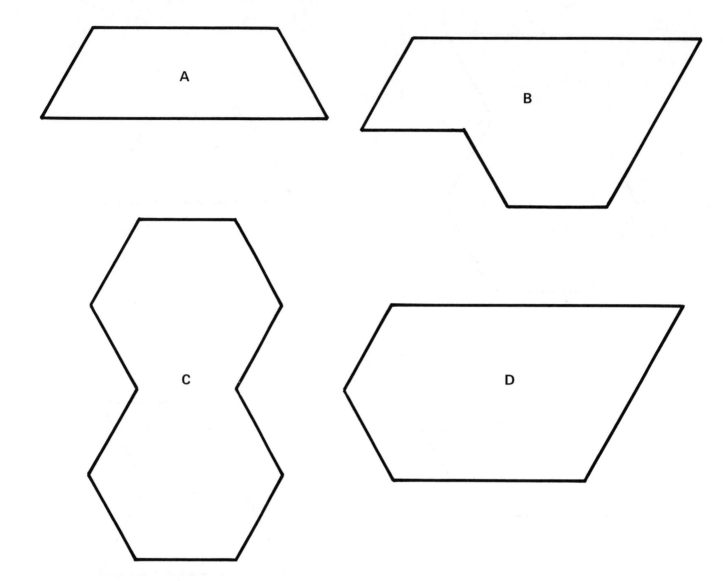

1)   IF "A" = 1   THEN   "B" =   "C" =   "D" =

2)   IF "B" = 1   THEN   "A" =   "C" =   "D" =

3)   IF "C" = 1   THEN   "A" =   "B" =   "D" =

4)   IF "D" = 1   THEN   "A" =   "B" =   "C" =

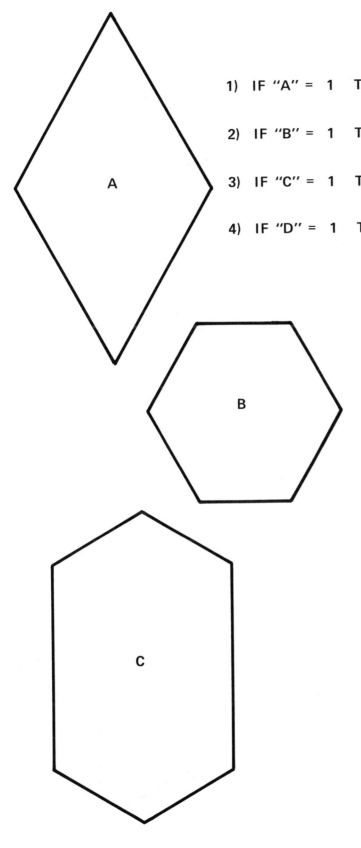

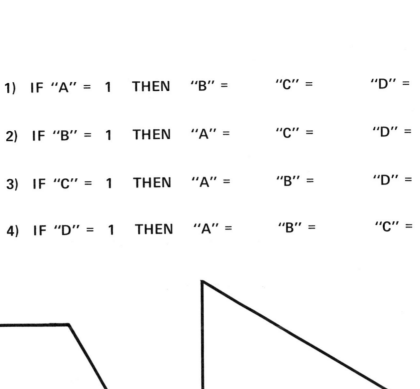

1) IF "A" = 1   THEN   "B" =   "C" =   "D" =

2) IF "B" = 1   THEN   "A" =   "C" =   "D" =

3) IF "C" = 1   THEN   "A" =   "B" =   "D" =

4) IF "D" = 1   THEN   "A" =   "B" =   "C" =

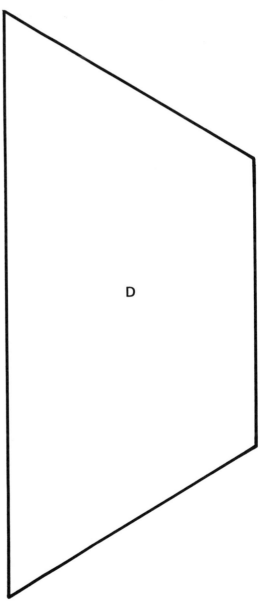

151

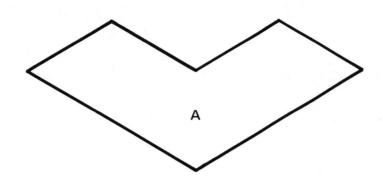

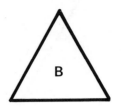

1) IF "A" = 1   THEN   "B" =   "C" =   "D" =

2) IF "B" = 1   THEN   "A" =   "C" =   "D" =

3) IF "C" = 1   THEN   "A" =   "B" =   "D" =

4) IF "D" = 1   THEN   "A" =   "B" =   "C" =

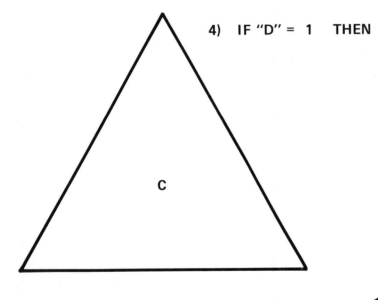

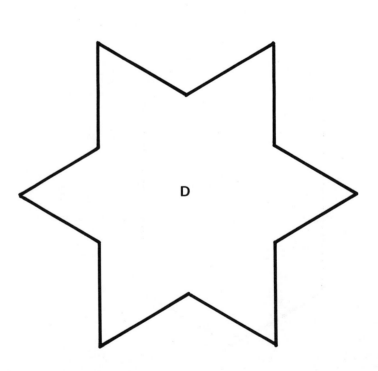

1) IF "A" = 1   THEN   "B" =   "C" =   "D" =

2) IF "B" = 1   THEN   "A" =   "C" =   "D" =

3) IF "C" = 1   THEN   "A" =   "B" =   "D" =

4) IF "D" = 1   THEN   "A" =   "B" =   "C" =

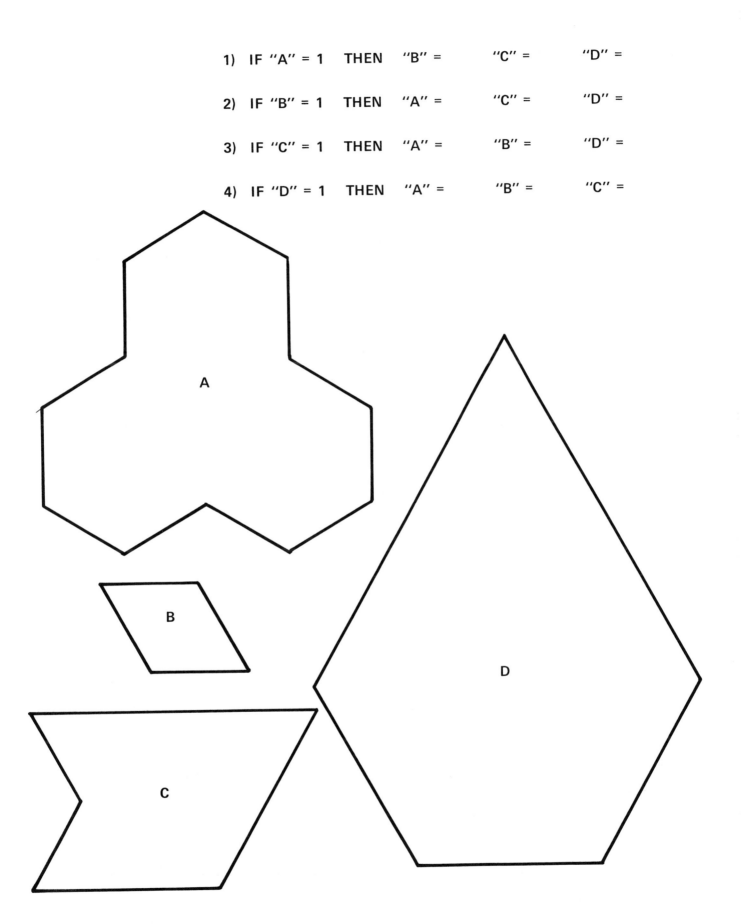

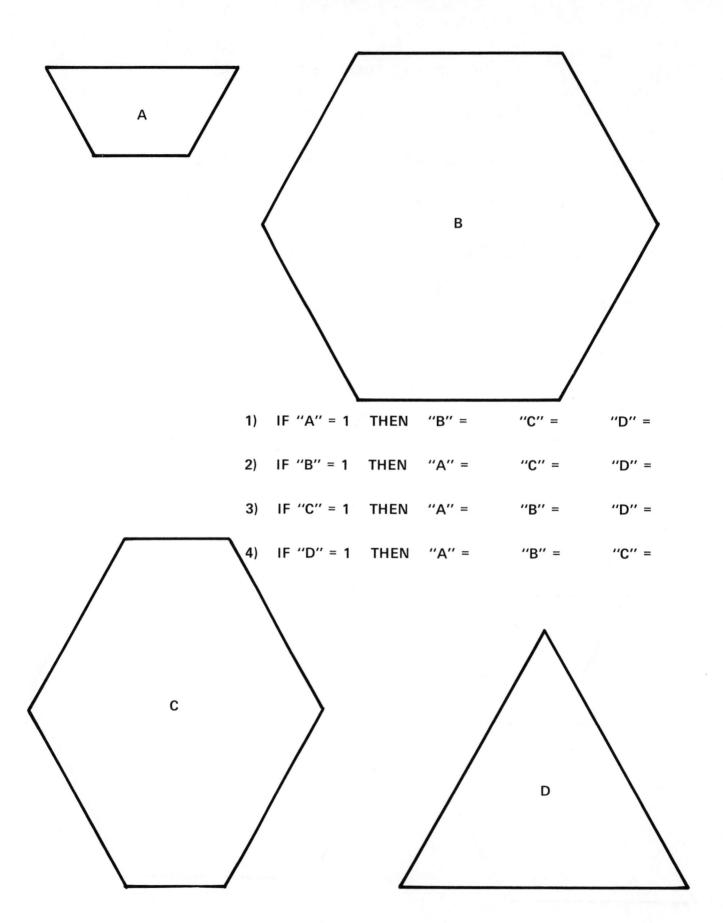

1) IF "A" = 1   THEN   "B" =   "C" =   "D" =

2) IF "B" = 1   THEN   "A" =   "C" =   "D" =

3) IF "C" = 1   THEN   "A" =   "B" =   "D" =

4) IF "D" = 1   THEN   "A" =   "B" =   "C" =

1)   IF "A" = 1   THEN   "B" =   "C" =   "D" =

2)   IF "B" = 1   THEN   "A" =   "C" =   "D" =

3)   IF "C" = 1   THEN   "A" =   "B" =   "D" =

4)   IF "D" = 1   THEN   "A" =   "B" =   "C" =

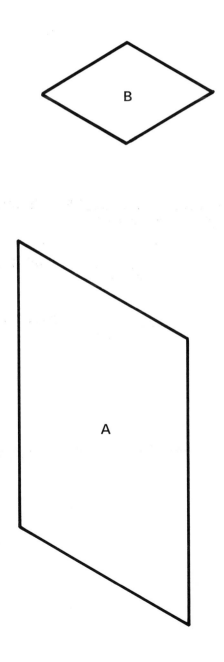

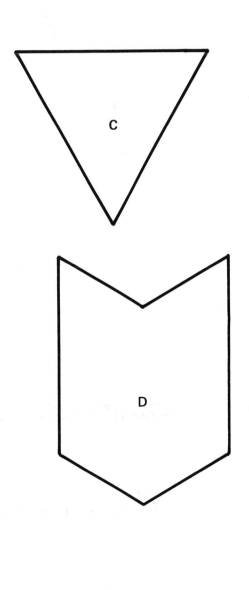

155

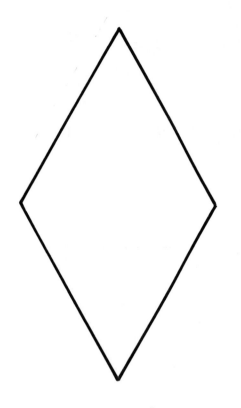

FILL THE SHAPE WITH BLOCKS OF THE
FOLLOWING COLORS: GREEN, BLUE,
AND RED. (YOU MUST USE AT LEAST
ONE BLOCK OF EACH COLOR)

GREEN IS＿＿＿＿＿＿＿OF THIS SHAPE.
          (WHAT FRACTION)

BLUE IS＿＿＿＿＿＿＿OF THIS SHAPE.
        (WHAT FRACTION)

RED IS ＿＿＿＿＿＿＿OF THIS SHAPE.
       (WHAT FRACTION)

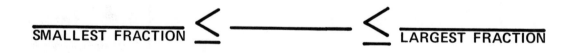

SMALLEST FRACTION $\leq$ ——— $\leq$ LARGEST FRACTION

$\leq$ MEANS LESS THAN OR EQUAL

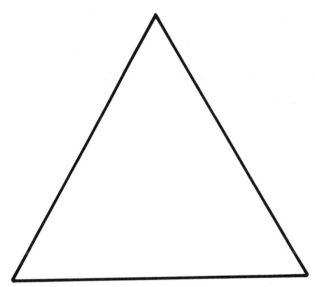

FILL THE SHAPE WITH BLOCKS OF THE
FOLLOWING COLORS: GREEN, BLUE,
AND RED. (YOU MUST USE AT LEAST
ONE BLOCK OF EACH COLOR)

GREEN IS_____OF THIS SHAPE.
　　　　　　(WHAT FRACTION)

BLUE IS _____OF THIS SHAPE.
　　　　　　(WHAT FRACTION)

RED IS _____OF THIS SHAPE.
　　　　　　(WHAT FRACTION)

SMALLEST FRACTION ≤ ———— ≤ LARGEST FRACTION

≤ MEANS LESS THAN OR EQUAL

FILL THE SHAPE WITH BLOCKS OF THE
FOLLOWING COLORS: GREEN, BLUE,
AND RED. (YOU MUST USE AT LEAST
ONE BLOCK OF EACH COLOR)

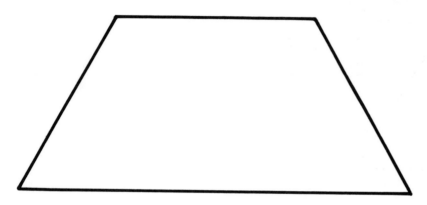

GREEN IS＿＿＿＿＿＿＿＿OF THIS SHAPE.
(WHAT FRACTION)

BLUE IS＿＿＿＿＿＿＿＿OF THIS SHAPE.
(WHAT FRACTION)

RED IS ＿＿＿＿＿＿＿＿OF THIS SHAPE.
(WHAT FRACTION)

SMALLEST FRACTION ≤ ——— ≤ LARGEST FRACTION

≤ MEANS LESS THAN OR EQUAL

FILL THE SHAPE WITH BLOCKS OF THE
FOLLOWING COLORS: GREEN, BLUE, RED,
AND YELLOW. (YOU MUST USE AT LEAST
ONE BLOCK OF EACH COLOR.)

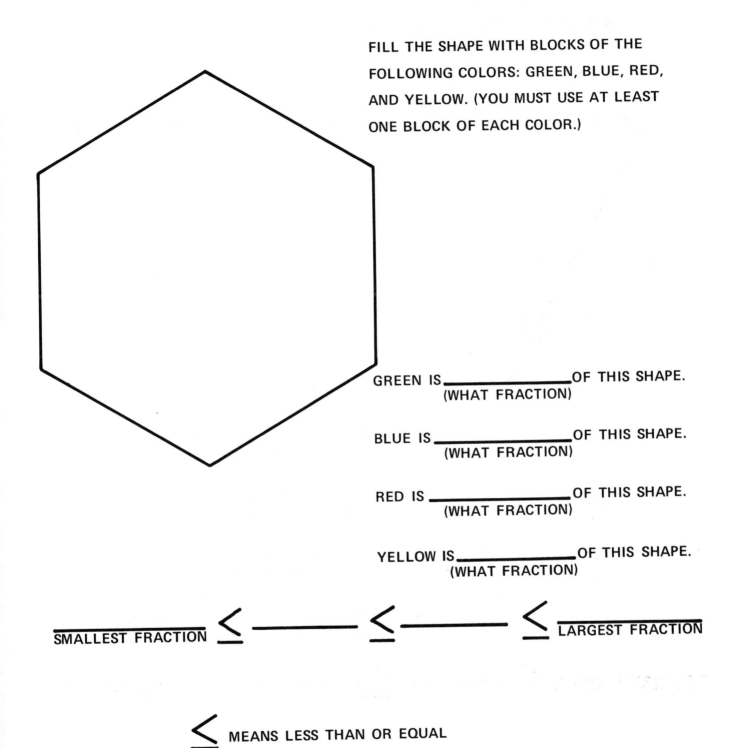

GREEN IS _____ OF THIS SHAPE.
(WHAT FRACTION)

BLUE IS _____ OF THIS SHAPE.
(WHAT FRACTION)

RED IS _____ OF THIS SHAPE.
(WHAT FRACTION)

YELLOW IS _____ OF THIS SHAPE.
(WHAT FRACTION)

SMALLEST FRACTION $\leq$ _____ $\leq$ _____ $\leq$ LARGEST FRACTION

$\leq$ MEANS LESS THAN OR EQUAL

FILL THE SHAPE WITH BLOCKS OF THE
FOLLOWING COLORS: GREEN, BLUE, RED,
AND YELLOW. (YOU MUST USE AT LEAST
ONE BLOCK OF EACH COLOR.)

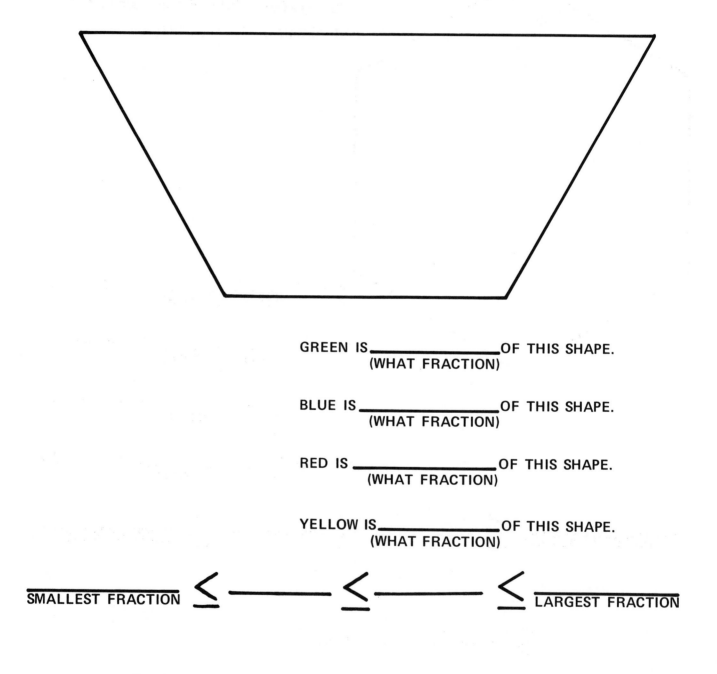

GREEN IS _____ OF THIS SHAPE.
        (WHAT FRACTION)

BLUE IS _____ OF THIS SHAPE.
        (WHAT FRACTION)

RED IS _____ OF THIS SHAPE.
        (WHAT FRACTION)

YELLOW IS _____ OF THIS SHAPE.
        (WHAT FRACTION)

SMALLEST FRACTION ≤ _____ ≤ _____ ≤ LARGEST FRACTION

≤ MEANS LESS THAN OR EQUAL

DAISY STRATEGY

HOW MANY BLOCKS COVER THE DAISY?

1	2	3	4	5	6	7	8	9	10
11	12	13	14	15	16	17	18	19	20
21	22	23	24	25	26	27	28	29	30
31	32	33	34	35	36	37	38	39	40

BLOCK JACK ACTIVITY (BIG TEN)

PLAYERS: Three to six with one player being the dealer.

EQUIPMENT NEEDED: 40 Blocks — 10 of each color, (green, blue, red, yellow) Also something for the dealer to hide from players the deck of blocks.

POINT VALUE OF BLOCKS: Green = 1   Blue = 2   Red = 3   Yellow = 6
(AREA VALUE)

OBJECT OF ACTIVITY: To score 10 or closest to ten than any of the other players without going over 10.

PLAY: To begin play the dealer mixes the 40 blocks and places them in a neat row with each block standing on one edge. (This is called the deck) These blocks should not be seen by the players.

The dealer deals (gives) each player 1 block from the deck.

Sample Game

1st DEAL   PLAYER "A"   PLAYER "B"   PLAYER "C"
                      1   2   6

The players then decide if they would like a second block knowing their score and the goal of ten.

2nd DEAL   PLAYER "A"   PLAYER "B"   PLAYER "C"
                   1   3   2   3   6   6
                  SCORE 4   SCORE 5   SCORE 12

Player "C" has 12 points now and cannot win game since he went past ten.

3rd DEAL   PLAYER "A"   PLAYER "B"   PLAYER "C"
                  1   3   2   2   3   6   6
                                          3
                  SCORE 6   SCORE 8   SCORE 12

4th DEAL   Player "B" did not want another block this deal, he passed. Once a player passes he cannot receive anymore blocks.

                  PLAYER "A"   PLAYER "B"   PLAYER "C"
                  1 3 2   2 3 3   6   6
                     3
                  SCORE 9   SCORE 8   SCORE 12

Player "A" is the winner of the 1st Game.

The dealer now mixes the 9 blocks that were played in game #1 and places them at the end of the deck.

The first player to win two games may become the dealer or select the next dealer. If a tie occurs each player declared the winner.

162

RHOMBUS Z

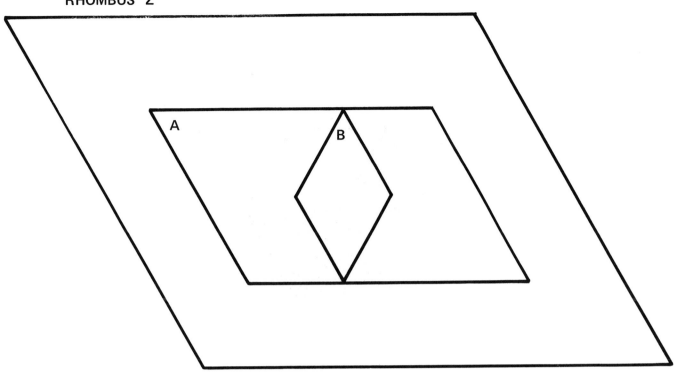

Z = 1

1.   A =

2.   B =

3.   Z — A =

4.   Z — B =

5.   A — B =

6.   IS "A" INSIDE "Z"?

7.   IS "B" INSIDE "A"?

8.   IS "B" INSIDE "Z"?

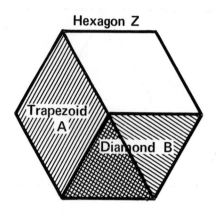

Z= 1

1.)   TRAPEZOID "A" = _____

2.)   DIAMOND "B" = _____

3.)   AUB = _____

4.)   Z—A = _____

5.)   Z—B = _____

6.)   THE PART SHARED BY "A" AND "B" IS _____

7.)   THE PART OF "A" NOT SHARED BY "B" IS _____

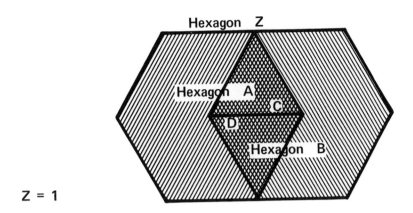

Z = 1

1.)　C = _____

2.)　D = _____

3.)　A = _____

4.)　B = _____

5.)　AUB = _____

6.)　CUD = _____

7.)　A − C = _____

8.)　A − D = _____

9.)　B − C = _____

10.)　THE PART SHARED BY "A" AND "B" IS _____

11.)　THE PART OF "A" WHICH IS NOT SHARED BY "B" IS _____

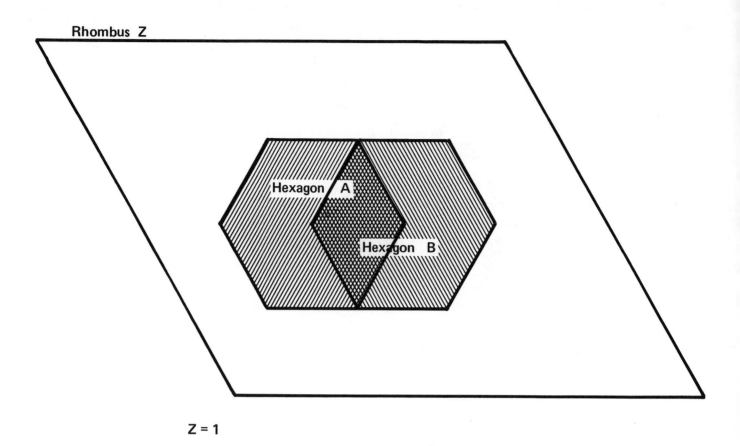

Rhombus Z

Hexagon A

Hexagon B

Z = 1

1.) A = _____

2.) B = _____

3.) Z − A = _____

4.) Z − B = _____

5.) A∪B = _____

6.) THE PART SHARED BY "A" AND "B" IS _____

7.) THE PART OF "A" WHICH IS NOT SHARED WITH "B" IS _____

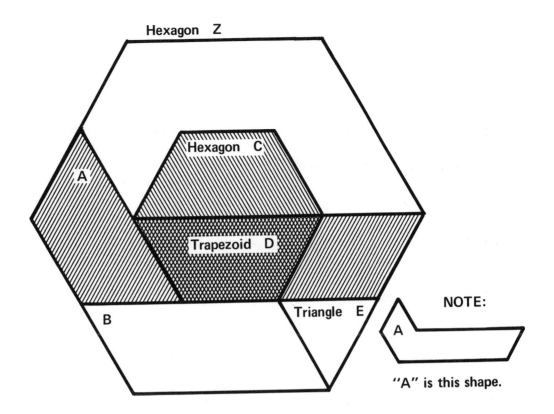

Hexagon Z

Hexagon C

A

Trapezoid D

B

Triangle E

NOTE:

A

"A" is this shape.

Z = 1

1.) A = _____

2.) B = _____

3.) C = _____

4.) D = _____

5.) E = _____

6.) AUB = _____

7.) AUE = _____

8.) AUBUE = _____

9.) Z − C = _____

10.) Z − D = _____

11.) Z − A = _____

12.) Z − B = _____

13.) Z − E = _____

14.) AUC = _____

15.) THE PART SHARED BY "A" AND

"C" IS _____

16.) THE PART SHARED BY "A" AND

"D" IS _____

BLOCK JACK RETURNS ACTIVITY (BIG 17)

This game is played with the same rules and equipment as Block Jack with the following exceptions:

The blocks are now worth   Green = 3   Blue = 4   Red = 5   Yellow = 6
                                                              (Perimeter Value)

The goal is now 17 points or closest to 17 without going beyond 17.

The First Deal   Each player receives 2 blocks instead of 1.

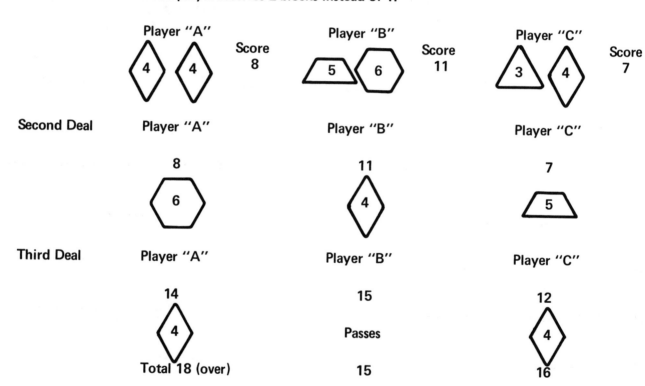

PLAYER "C" WINS

ANSWERS

Page 17.   From least (13) to maximum (36).

Page 43.   From least (8) to maximum (27).

Page 57.   A. Circle all numbers 1–12.
           B. Circle all numbers 1–8.

Page 58.   A. Circle 2–6, 8–11, 13.
           B. Circle 2–10, 12.

Page 59.   A. Circle 3, 6, 9, 12, 15, 18, 21, 24.
           B. Circle 3, 6, 9, 12, 15, 18, 21.

Page 98.   From least (7) to maximum (22).

Page 106. Ways to score 12 points:
           1) 6, 6
           2) 6, 3, 3
           3) 6, 3, 2, 1
           4) 6, 2, 2, 2
           5) 3, 3, 3, 3
           6) 3, 3, 2, 2, 2
           7) 2, 2, 2, 2, 2, 2

           Half the ways to score 18:
           1) 6, 6, 6,
           2) 6, 6, 3, 3
           3) 6, 6, 3, 2, 1
           4) 6, 6, 2, 2, 2
           5) 6, 6, 2, 2, 1, 1
           6) 6, 3, 3, 3, 3
           7) 6, 3, 3, 3, 2, 1

Page 138. 1) 2, 3, 6
           2) 4, 6, 12
           3) 6, 9, 18
           4) 20, 30, 60
           5) 200, 300, 600

Page 139. 1) 4, 6, 2
           2) 2, 3, 1
           3) 1, 3/2, 3/6 or ½
           4) 4/6 or 2/3, 1, 2/6 or 1/3
           5) 2/6 or 1/3, ½, 1/6

Page 140. 1) 1, 3/2, 3
           2) 2/3, 1, 2
           3) 2/4 or ½, 3/4, 6/4 or 3/2
           4) 2/5, 3/5, 6/5
           5/ 2/6 or 1/3, 3/6 or ½, 1

Page 141. 1) .2, .3, .6
           2) .4, .6, 1.2
           3) .6, .9, 1.8
           4) .8, 1.2, 2.4
           5) 1.4, 2.1, 4.2

Page 142. 1) 75, 150, 25
           2) 30, 60, 10
           3) 15, 30, 5
           4) 3, 6, 1
           5) 3/2, 3, ½

Page 143. 1) 20, 10, 60
           2) 2/5, 1/5, 6/5
           3) 2/100 or 1/50, 1/10, 6/10 or 3/5
           4) 2/6 or 1/3, 1/6, 1
           5) 2/12 or 1/6, 1/12, 2/4 or ½

Page 144. Top: 3/2, 2/3
           Bottom: 5/6, 6/5

Page 145. Top: 5/6, 6/5
           Bottom: 3/10, 10/3

Page 146. 1) 2/6 or 1/3, 2/3
           2) 3, 2
           3) 3/2, ½

Page 147. 1) 24, 36, 72
           2) 6, 18, 36
           3) 4, 8, 24
           4) 2, 4, 6
           5) 144, 216, 432
           6) 36, 108, 216
           7) 24, 48, 144
           8) 12, 24, 36

Page 148. 1) 2, 3, 6
           2) ½, 3/2, 3
           3) 1/3, 2/3, 2
           4) 1/6, 2/6 or 1/3, ½

Page 149. 1) 1/3 or 3/9, 4/9, 5/9
           2) 3, 4/3, 5/3
           3) 9/4, 3/4, 5/4
           4) 9/5, 3/5, 4/5

Page 150. 1) 9/5, 12/5, 11/5
           2) 5/9, 12/9 or 4/3, 11/9
           3) 5/12, 9/12 or ¾, 11/12
           4) 5/11, 9/11, 12/11

Page 151. 1) 6/8 or ¾, 10/8 or 5/4, 27/8
           2) 8/6 or 4/3, 10/6 or 5/3, 6/27 or 2/9
           3) 8/10 or 4/5, 6/10 or 3/5, 10/27
           4) 8/27, 27/6 or 9/2, 27/10

Page 152. 1) 1/6, 9/6 or 3/2, 12/6 or 2
           2) 6, 9, 12
           3) 6/9 or 2/3, 1/9, 12/9 or 4/3
           4) 6/12 or ½, 1/12, 9/12 or ¾

Page 153. 1) 2/18 or 1/9, 9/18 or ½, 28/18 or 14/9
           2) 18/2 or 9, 9/2, 28/2 or 14
           3) 18/9 or 2, 2/9, 28/9
           4) 18/28 or 9/14, 2/28 or 1/14, 9/28

Page 154. 1) 24/3 or 8, 16/3, 9/3 or 3
           2) 3/24 or 1/8, 16/24 or 2/3, 9/24 or 3/8
           3) 3/16, 24/16 or 3/2, 9/16
           4) 3/9 or 1/3, 24/9 or 8/3, 16/9

ANSWERS

Page 155. 1) 2/12 or 1/6, 4/12 or 1/3, 8/12 or 2/3
2) 12/2 or 6, 4/2 or 2, 8/2 or 4
3) 12/4 or 3, 2/4 or 1/2, 8/4 or 2
4) 12/8 or 3/2, 2/8 or 1/4, 4/8 or 1/2

Page 163. 1) 12/40 or 3/10
2) 2/40 or 1/20
3) 28/40 or 7/10
4) 38/40 or 19/20
5) 10/40 or 1/4
6) yes
7) yes
8) yes

Page 164. 1) 3/6 or ½
2) 2/6 or 1/3
3) 4/6 or 2/3
4) 3/6 or ½
5) 4/6 or 2/3
6) 1/6
7) 2/6 or 1/3

Page 165. 1) 1/10
2) 1/10
3) 6/10 or 3/5
4) 6/10 or 3/5
5) 10/10 or 1
6) 2/10 or 1/5
7) 5/10 or ½
8) 5/10 or ½
9) 5/10 or ½
10) 2/10 or 1/5
11) 4/10 or 2/5

Page 166. 1) 6/40 or 3/20
2) 6/40 or 3/20
3) 34/40 or 17/20
4) 34/40 or 17/20
5) 10/40 or ¼
6) 2/40 or 1/20
7) 4/40 or 1/10

Page 167. 1) 8/24 or 1/3
2) 4/24 or 1/6
3) 6/24 or 1/4
4) 3/24 or 1/8
5) 1/24
6) 12/24 or ½
7) 9/24 or 3/8
8) 13/24
9) 18/24 or 3/4
10) 21/24 or 7/8
11) 16/24 or 2/3
12) 20/24 or 5/6
13) 23/24
14) 11/24
15) 3/24 or 1/8
16) 3/24 or 1/8